CULTURAL DIVERSITY IN LIBRARIES

Edited by

Donald E. Riggs

Patricia A. Tarin

Neal-Schuman Publishers, Inc.
New York   London

MAR 0 7 1996

Published by Neal-Schuman Publishers, Inc.
100 Varick Street
New York, NY 10013

Printed and bound in the United States of America

Library of Congress Cataloging-in-Publication Data

Cultural diversity in libraries / [edited by] Donald E. Riggs and
    Patricia A. Tarin .
        p.   cm.
    Includes bibliographical references (p .) and index.
    ISBN 1-55570-139-6
    1.   University of Michigan. Library--Administration.   2. Academic
libraries--Michigan--Administration--Case studies.
3. Multiculturalism--Michigan--Case studies.   4. Libraries and
minorities--Michigan--Case Studies.   I. Riggs , Donald E.
II. Tarin , Patricia A.
Z733.U859C85   1994
025 . 1'9774'35--dc20   94-17007
                                                            CIP

Contents

Preface

For the past few years, the University of Michigan Library
has actively made diversity a vital part of its culture. Its efforts have focused on a comprehensive effort, striving for
diversity in collections, staff, and services. In 1991, the
University recognized the Library as having "A Model
Diversity Program," and selected it for the University's first
Affirmative Action Award.

Making cultural diversity a reality in libraries requires a
change in mind set, an understanding that the U.S. society
is inherently pluralistic. What multiculturalism means for
libraries must be carefully defined and well-articulated
throughout the library. Cultural diversity must be reflected
in a library's vision statement, mission, and goals; it must
be included in the library's strategic planning process.

The diversity revolution should be welcomed as an opportunity, as a challenge to improve all aspects of the
library. Librarians should not only welcome the concept of
diversity, but should take the initiative in making it a reality. Rather than just reacting to external mandates, librarians should make a personal commitment to cultural
diversity. An investment in diversity is necessary if a
library's management is going to walk the diversity talk.

The University of Michigan Library staff has made a
genuine commitment to its diversity efforts. We have
experienced many successes, but our diversity endeavor is
still evolving. One purpose of this book is to share with
other libraries our many diversity activities that are becoming the norm rather than the unusual.

All contributors are either currently or formerly employed by the University of Michigan. Special thanks are extended to Patricia Tarin for assisting with the identification of contributors and to June Corkin for her able revising and editing assistance. This book is dedicated to Sallie Dettling who spent many hours typing and re-typing the manuscript.

All royalty income received from the sale of this book will be given to the University of Michigan Library's Diversity Committee for its activities.

—DONALD E. RIGGS

Introduction

A multicultural environment reflects and responds to the real world by understanding and respecting one's fellow human beings in ways that are meaningful to each individual. People cannot work productively and pursue knowledge where their dignity is denied by demands to conform to a standard that, by definition, excludes them. According to Stephen R. Covey, an authority on personal organizational leadership, "Each of us tends to think we see things as they are, that we are objective—but this is not the case. We see the world, not as it is, but as we are—or, as we are conditioned to see it. When we open our mouths to describe what we see, we in effect describe ourselves, our perceptions, our paradigms. When other people disagree with us, we immediately think something is wrong with them . . . sincere, clearheaded people see things differently, each looking through the unique lense of experience."[1]

Regardless of the outcome of the intellectual battles raging over multiculturalism, libraries will be involved in its pursuit. As they exist to seek out and impartially present differing viewpoints, libraries serve persons from the whole spectrum.

If the ideal of free speech is to have all ideas and points of view heard, diversity is the embodiment of that ideal. It follows that diversity in the library is as basic as free speech. Whether addressing people or ideas, society is not well-served when the *fact* of variety and differences is ignored. Individuals who acknowledge nothing beyond their own culturally rooted view of the world limit their ca-

capacity for knowledge and understanding. If they do not learn about others, they cannot truly know themselves.

Cultural Diversity in Libraries is intended to help libraries effectively perform their mission as a resource for knowledge covering the widest possible range of perspectives. The University of Michigan Library staff has spent the past few years exploring what it means to serve and work with increasing numbers of people who are not from the dominant cultural milieu. The distillation of their experience forms the basis for this book.

The road they have taken has not been easy, nor has it been universally appreciated. Some within the campus community and the Library preferred the comfort of the status quo predicated upon an often illusionary homogeneous environment. Whether this environment ever actually existed, it certainly does not exist now. Just as taxation without representation was intolerable over two hundred years ago, education without inclusion is unrealistic today.

Whether one agrees or vehemently disagrees that there is only one clearly distinct and true American culture, librarians are bound by their profession to offer all evidence to the contrary, to present all sides of the issue. Librarians are educated to value the individual, to deplore labeling, particularly when isolated incidents are exaggerated to create false impressions about groups of people.

To deny that there is a need to eradicate racism, sexism, and homophobia is to be tolerant of the intolerable. Tolerance is a luxury for those who do not suffer abuse or lack basic human rights. Luxury should come after necessity, not before. The conflict between free speech and civil rights (as if they were somehow diametrically opposed) is not new to librarians. When one values the concepts that all ideas have an equal right to be expressed *and* that all people are equal and have the right to be protected from indignity and hatred, a collision is inevitable.

This clash of values is constantly played out in libraries with both sides claiming some victories and defeats. The classic example of this is the controversy over the film "The Speaker." Is it possible to believe deeply in freedom of speech and still wish to protect a group of people from hatred or harassment? For many, the rights of people are paramount. For others, freedom of speech does not allow for exceptions. Both values have incredible worth, but the problems raised in their application require the wisdom of Solomon to resolve. The functional result is an issue-by-issue accommodation where the same players may frequently change sides as individual issues develop. The free speech vs. diversity conflict will continue to take center stage on campuses and in the broader society as long as there is a fascination with issues that allow each side to be so right and still so wrong.

Meanwhile, to stay competitive in the world economy, our society educates increasing numbers of minorities and white women. Recognizing and meeting their information needs as students and scholars is a crucial activity for librarians, regardless of their individual opinions. This book begins to provide some tested tools for doing this. The authors speak from their experiences in involving and recruiting a staff reflective of a culturally diverse workplace, and providing collections, services, and programs supportive of a diverse clientele. In evaluating their problems as well as their triumphs, they present the essence of their findings with a candor that should be useful to other libraries wishing to increase their diversity efforts.

REFERENCES

1. Stephen R. Covey, *The Seven Habits of Highly Effective People,* (New York: Simon and Schuster, 1989), p. 28.

—PATRICIA TARIN

1

Perspectives on Cultural Diversity

Vivian Sykes

When asked to speak about cultural diversity, I think of the songs I hum in my head. The songs blend new age wisdom with Brazilian percussion, Native American flutes, South African folk tunes, inner city rap, and country music's fiddle. For me, multiculturalism goes beyond trends and statistics; for me, diversity has a human face.

In part, this chapter reflects the movement toward diversity within academic libraries. It also is written to remind us of the humanity beyond the impersonal numbers and institutional categories in which we fit people to fulfill goals and measure achievement. The issues of diversity and ways of achieving it within librarianship are not new; yet in earlier days, the philosophies driving diversity appeared more humanistic and people-oriented than our present day efforts.

TRENDS AND SUCH

Since the 1960s, diversifying the profession of librarianship has been an issue.[1] To confront the traditional barriers created by ethnicity, gender, race, and sexual preference, organizations such as the American Library Association's Social Responsibilities Round Table, ethnic caucuses, gay and lesbian task forces, and feminist task forces have defined strategies for addressing these issues in the numerous facets of librarianship. Such endeavors have helped keep diversity awareness alive within ALA and its many divisions. But have these efforts given us the statistical and structural changes that should have occurred within the profession? Have they adequately prepared academic librarianship for the approaching year 2000? What statistical and demographic trends can guide us in dealing with these issues?

WORK FORCE 2000

Cultural diversity became a prominent news topic in the latter 1980s and early 1990s as demographic statistics began to match predicted trends. The changing demographics forced institutions in the United States to re-think hiring policies.[2] *American Demographer* predicted dramatic population shifts from 1980 to 2000. The greatest gains and shifts have occurred in the Southwest and the West.[3] In many areas, changing populations have already altered the texture of hiring practices. Many major cities throughout the United States no longer have white majorities. Within the Southwest and the West, many cities are dominated by cultural and ethnic groups.[4]

One major published piece that forced work places to stand and take notice was *Work Force 2000*. This study predicted that, by the year 2000, there will be a dramatic increase in the number of women and minorites entering the work force. Women will also make up 47 percent of the general work force.[5] Private organizations have responded with extensive recruiting efforts to make sure their staffs will represent the ever-changing hiring populations. They have also used cultural training workshops to teach skills that few people receive during their basic education. Both these efforts ensure that supervisors will be sensitive to the people they hire and supervise.[6]

LIBRARIES AND TRENDS

The library world was not idle while these predictions and changes were being made. Many workshops and pre-conferences prepared the various parts of librarianship for these shifts.[7] One major pre-conference resulting in a policy paper was held at the 1988 ALA New Orleans Annual Conference. The final paper, "Librarians in the New Millenium," tackled many diversity and recruitment issues within the profession.[8] Some other subjects covered were

1. The general recruitment pool,
2. Minority recruitment,
3. Catalogers, and
4. Academic librarians.

Since 1988, an increasing body of literature within librarianship have embraced and reviewed the issue of diversity.[9] Diversity and its facets has not come easily into a profession in which men hold the major leadership positions over a predominately female staff.[10] Although the largest number of librarians (73.15 percent) are women, they have problems reaching managerial roles.[11]

Divisions of ALA (e.g., Association of College and Research Libraries and the Library Administration and Management Association) have become more concerned about issues of diversity and recruitment and how the profession can meet the challenge. In ACRL, committees and task forces have developed guidelines for assisting academic libraries with recruitment assessment.[12] ACRL's College & Research Libraries and *C&RL News* have run regular articles on diversity. The ACRL Racial and Ethnic Diversity Committee has sponsored a column *C&RL News*.[13]

The profession is changing and ALA's efforts are greater than ever. Each year, more ALA divisions tackle these issues. The number of programs on diversity at ALA annual conferences and midwinter meetings underscore the concerted efforts being made to explore and address diversity issues. ALA units are not alone. Individual libraries, such as those of the University of Michigan, are also rising to attack and solve diversity issues.

THE UNIVERSITY OF MICHIGAN AND DIVERSITY

The University of Michigan began a herculean diversity program in March of 1988.[14] Recognizing that an effective response to demographic statistics and trends had to go beyond mere access, UM strove to change the institution's cultural and structural perspectives. As a result, the University of Michigan Library saw a significant increase in minority librarians during a seven-year period.[15]

YEAR	TOTAL # OF LIBRARIANS	% OF MINORITY
1985	115	13
1986	102	19
1987	105	18
1988	105	20
1989	105	21.9
1990	100	22
1991	109	22
1992	108	21.3

According to the ALA's Office for Library Personnel Resources, the number of minority librarians in academic libraries increased 17.2 percent from 1985 to 1991.[16]

1985

American Indian/Alaskan Native	.2%
Asian/Pacific Islander	4.5%
Black	4.1%
Hispanic	1.5%
Total minority representation	10.3%

1991

American Indian/Alaskan Native	.63%
Asian/Pacific Islander	4.95%
Black	4.96%
Hispanic	1.53%
Total minority representation	12.07%

As illustrated by comparing the 12.07 minority percent of librarians in academic libraries in 1991 with the 22 percent employed in the University of Michigan Library for the same year, the UM Library obviously did remarkably well in this area. The University of Michigan achieved its statistical success through numerous varied efforts. Recruitment efforts were revamped to creatively attract people. New pools of potential applicants were developed from research and library associates. Active recruitment at library schools, job fairs, and ALA, as well as consideration of public librarians for academic positions, also assisted. These recruitment efforts, combined with an ongoing, vigorous cultural diversity program, helped to retain people. Marketing the diversity program, incorporating the program into the Library's structure, developing special diversity librarian positions, formulating special programs for students of color, and having a Gay and Lesbian Task Force enabled the UM Library to improve its diversity.[17]

Implications of Trends Nationally and at The University of Michigan

American Demographer indicated that national and localized trends force agencies to think long-term about employment. By the year 2000, 38 percent of children under 18 will be children of color, and one out of three children will speak a language other than English. In addition, certain parts of the country's population will be 30 percent Chicano/Latino, 15 percent African American, 12 percent Asian/Pacific and 3 percent Native American.[18] Current librarian demographics do not represent this rapidly-changing population, and the statistics do not suggest, for example, how universities' staffs can become more reflective of their undergraduate student bodies and library users.[19]

The University of California at Berkeley conducted a major study on the impact of diversity on the campus community. The interim report presented various student definitions of diversity and its impact on their lives. Incorporating student viewpoints allowed the report to more fully suggest how ethnic classes and diversity requirements will change how libraries relate to the total campus.[20] Trends and statistics alone can not completely inform us about service and access issues, bibliographic instruction, reference services, and continued recruitment, promotion, and retention issues.

In recent years, we have seen articles on racism, cultural climate within libraries, affirmative action impact, retention, and diversity supervision and training.[21] These articles indicate that access to a job is not enough; institutional climate and structure must change to reflect the many cultures now within the American work force. These sticky issues nag at administrators and personnel officers. The issues cannot be easily addressed and will continue to pose challenges to people anticipating and planning for change. Trying to achieve change without a diversity committee supported and validated by an administration will prove hazardous to any academic institution.[22]

At risk are the realities we face within our society. Several articles examine the trend of rising racism and its impact on universities.[23] Libraries are not immune from racism and all of its related "isms." The film *Racism 101* depicts UM's own baptism by fire, documenting some of the virulent racial occurrences at the University during 1987 and 1988.

The low percentage of women making it to administrative supervisory roles is still of concern. Pay equity is still an issue. The ghettoization of women in the roles of school librarians and public librarians is still with us.[24] ALA's Committee on the Status of Women in Librarianship and the Feminist Task Force still fight to achieve more equable distributions. Overall statistics for OLPR in the last few years reveal little growth in the number of people of color at academic libraries.[25]

As impatience with the status quo grows, standard employment issues demand new evaluations. Will women continue to remain at companies that limit their advancement? Will a person of color remain if the climate permits daily frustrations to occur? In a March 1992 *Glamour* article, women of color said constant slights at work wore them down.[26] Will a gay person remain in a place where sexual preferences must be concealed? The human faces of diversity cannot be overshadowed by statistics and trends. Our institutions comprise people: people who must work together, communicate with one another, share some cultural similarities, appreciate cultural differences, create workable cultural climates, and serve the changing face of our diverse users.

Cultural Values of the Institution

Several years ago, trainers tried to get people of color and women to understand and accept the corporate culture and its personal implications. Trainers dictated dress codes, language nuances, cultural styles, and learning processes. They assumed that marginal persons would adjust their culture to the one at work.[27] Now, trainers and consultants suggest that the corporate culture change to reflect the many cultures brought to the job.[28] This presents short- and long-term training and design implications for academic libraries, as an absence of retention techniques can hollow successful recruitment techniques.

Retention becomes crucial as more professions compete for the same students of color. The maturation of the baby boomer generation leaves a dwindling minority pool of librarians, further frustrating recruitment efforts.[29] We, as librarians, actively compete with business, law, medical, and professional schools for students of color. We must refocus our recruitment efforts to innovatively attract people into librarianship. OLPR recommends addressing audiences younger than high school and college students, targeting elementary and junior high school students.

Challenges Facing the University of Michigan

The University faces the same concerns as the national profession. Where will we continue or begin to recruit? How will we recruit? How will we retain those we have? Will the corporate culture change to include other cultures within the hiring pool? What will be the impact of the changing economic structure within the State of Michigan? How will the issues of diversity compete with other issues within the library budget? Should libraries work with other organizations in recruitment? These and other questions cannot be ignored. Libraries must work more effectively within their universities to acquire resources for the recruitment, retention, and promotion of minorities and women on their staff.

Other issues that deserve attention include 1) the replacement of affirmative action with new equity efforts, 2) economic cut backs, factory closings, intra-regional population shifts, and immigration and related language needs, and 3) the changing student body.

A strong diversity program for the library would do the following:

1. Maintain the recruitment concept and broaden the geographical range of the net;
2. Continue validating and strengthening the roles of the committees and positions with diversity responsibilities;
3. Develop a mentor program to assist library support staff in becoming librarians;
4. Develop new access tools for identifying subsets of information on diversity;
5. Evaluate the atmosphere of support for multiculturalism;
6. Create new ways to interest children in librarianship;
7. Forge new links with library schools to examine diversity and its impact on libraries; and
8. Sponsor regional and national events on diversity in the year 2000 and the accompanying changes in libraries.

CONCLUSION

If we examine trends and statistics without looking at what they mean, we will hobble into 2000 without addressing the infrastructures that foment and support change. The challenge lies in accurately reading the demographic implications to create structures and relationships never before encountered in academic libraries. We hold the opportunity to forge new cultures, new communications, and new languages, to create an ongoing diversity quilt that will forever blend and enhance the many faces of our culture. Different voices breathe life into trends and statistics, giving them a "human face."

REFERENCES

1. Ann Randall, "Minority Recruitment in Librarianship," *Librarians for the New Millenium*, eds. William Moen and Kathleen Heim (Chicago: American Library Association, Office for Library Personnel Resources, 1988), pp. 11-25.

   Donnarae MacCann, ed., *Social Responsibilities in Librarianship: Essays in Equality* (Jefferson, NC: McFarland, 1989).

   E. J. Josey, ed., *The Information Society: Issues and Answers* (Phoenix: Oryx Press, 1978).

   Patricia Schuman, "Social Responsibility: A Progress Report," *Library Journal*, 114 (1989), pp. 12-18.
2. Judith Waldrop, "2010," *American Demographer*, 11 (1989), p. 18.

   Judith Waldrop and Thomas Exter, "What the 1990 Census Will Show," *American Demographer*, 12 (1990), pp. 20-30.
3. *Ibid.* p. 24, p. 26.
4. *Ibid.* pp. 24-25.
5. *Opportunity 2000: Creative Affirmative Action Strategies for a Changing Workforce* (Indianapolis: Hudson Institute, 1988).
6. Marcus Mabry et al., "Past Tokenism," *Newsweek* (May 14, 1990), pp. 37-43.

   Benson Rosen and Kay Lovelace, "Piecing Together the Diversity Puzzle," *HR Magazine*, 36 (1991)pp. 78-82.

   The Challenge of Diversity: Equal Employment Opportunity and Managing Differences in the 1990's (Washington, D.C.: BNA Communications, July 1991).
7. Kathleen Heim, "Librarians for the New Millenium," *Librarians for the New Millenium*, eds. William Loen and Kathleen Heim. (Chicago: ALA/OLPR, 1988), pp. 1-10.
8. *Ibid.* p.1.
9. Vivian Sykes, *Unpublished Bibliography on Cultural Diversity and Its Impact on Libraries*, (Produced for the Arizona Chapter of Association of College and Research Libraries regional meeting, April, 1991).
10. Kathleen Heim, *Career Profiles and Sex Discrimination in the Library Profession* (Chicago: ALA, 1983), p.38.
11. Sarah M. Pritchard, "The Impact of Feminism on Women in the Profession," *Library Journal*, 114 (13) (1989), pp. 76-77.

    Suzanne Hildebrand, "Women's Work Within Librarianship: Time to Expand the Feminist Agenda," *Library Journal*, 114 (14) (1989), pp. 153-155.
12. ACRL Task Force on Recruitment of Underrepresented Minorities, "Recruiting the Underrepresented to Academic Libraries," *C&RL News*, 51 (1990), p. 1016.

13. *Ibid.* p. 1018.
14. *Point of Intersection: The University Library and the Pluralistic Campus Community* (Ann Arbor: The University of Michigan Library, November 28, 1988).
    Point of Intersection II: The University Library Moves Toward Diversity (June 1990).
15. University of Michigan, Office of Personnel, report on the distribution of staff by race for 1985-1992.
16. *Academic and Public Librarians: Data by Race, Ethnicity and Sex* (Chicago: ALA/OLPR, April 1991), Table 3.
17. Assorted University of Michigan documents including Point of Intersection reports.
18. Joe Schwartz and Thomas Exter, "All Our Children," *American Demographics,* 11 (1989), pp. 34-37.
19. *The Diversity Project: An Interim Report to the Chancellor* (University of California, Berkeley: Institute for the Study of Social Change, June 1990).
20. *The Many Voices of Diversity: Report of the AdHoc Committee on Librarian Association of University of California, Regional Workshops on Cultural Diversity in Libraries* (University of California, Berkeley: Librarian Association of University of California, 1992).
21. The entire issue of *Library Administration and Management,* 5 (1991) focuses on "Serving Diverse Client Groups."
22. Rhonda Rios Kravitz et al., "Serving the Emerging Majority: Documenting Their Voices," *Library Administration and Management,* 5 (1991), pp. 184-188.
23. Patrick Hall, "Yassuh! I's the Reference Librarian," *American Libraries,* 19 (1988), pp. 900-901.
    Elizabeth Martinez Smith, "Racism: It's Always There," *Library Journal,* 113 (1988), pp. 35-39.
    Jan S. Squire, "Job Satisfaction and the Ethnic Minority Librarian," *Library Administration and Management,* 5 (1991), p. 194.
24. Sarah Pritchard, loc. cit.
25. *Academic and Public Librarians: Data by Race, Ethnicity and Sex for 1991,* (Chicago: ALA/OLPR, 1991).
26. Martha Southgate, "Women of Color: On the Frontlines of a Changing Workplace," *Glamour,* (March, 1992), p. 224.
27. Marcus Mabry et al., op. cit., p. 37
28. *Glamour,* (March, 1992), p. 271.
29. Kathleen Heim, "Librarians for the New Millenium," p. 1.

2

Moving to Diversity: Institutional Philosophy and Role

Carla J. Stoffle

Throughout American history, cyclical social movements have focused on the need to provide a more equitable society, especially in terms of race and gender. The Constitution officially recognized the legitimacy of this goal. The Fourteenth Amendment provided for equal protection under the law, and the Nineteenth Amendment gave women the right to vote. For the most part, early "equitable society" movements based their appeal on morality and altruism. The call was to treat people equally because it was the right thing to do.

In the 1960s, America's social consciousness on race and gender issues reached another peak as moralism and legal remedies to date ran out of steam. Proponents of the equitable society accepted that morality and altruism were not enough to eliminate the barriers to full participation in all areas of American life for women and minorities. Additional laws in the form of Civil Rights legislation, voting rights, affirmative action, and equal employment opportunity supplemented previous legal remedies and their appeal to conscience. They sought to dismantle America's discrimination on the basis of race and gender through the legislation of people's behaviors and through large, rapid injections of women and minorities into the workplace.

The underlying philosophy presumed that personal attitudes and workplace climates could be subordinated and eventually transformed by regulated public behavior. It followed that, once in the workplace, women and people of color would advance, discrimination would melt away, and more people of color and women would be voluntarily hired. Familiarity would breed justice and equity. Equal employment opportunity and affirmative action guidelines and procedures would speed the integration of the private, as well as public, workplace and would shortly lead to an "equitable society." The legal remedies were temporary necessities to redress past wrongs and deficiencies.

The operant definition of affirmative action suggested that women or persons of color would be selected only when a prevailing criteria made all individuals equal. Equal employment opportunity further called for creating procedures giving everyone who was qualified an equal chance to know about and apply for a position. With the playing field leveled, integration would result.

Unfortunately, by the end of the 1980s, the legal remedies of the 1960s had, for the most part, failed. Even with hiring goals, tests, and criteria norming added to affirmative action procedures and requirements to actively seek "qualified candidates" appended to equal employment opportunity, women and minorities still had not moved into the workplace and positions of authority and decision-making in demographically proportional numbers. Racist, sexist, and homophobic incidents remained commonplace not only in the workplace, but also in the last bastion of social consciousness—college campuses. Reverse discrimination complaints and threats of lawsuits abounded. A widely publicized "political correctness" backlash insidiously attacked what gains were made. Women and minorities regularly faced hostile environments and remarks: "If you are a minority or woman and you apply, the job is yours." "Affirmative action hires are unqualified." "Any woman or minority hire is an affirmative action hire." "Whites are fired to hire minorities." A decade-ending American Council on Education report, *One Third of a Nation,* concluded that America is moving backward, not forward, in its efforts to achieve full participation of minority citizens in the life and prosperity of the nation.[1]

As the nation's prosperity takes on a new urgency, an equitable society needs to be created whereby women, people of color, the differently abled, lesbians, gays, etc. can enjoy full involvement in the workforce. By the year 2000, one-third of U.S. citizens will be from cultural and racial minority groups. Over 50 percent of the school age population in our 25 largest cities will be minorities. Over 45 percent of available workers will be women. The availability of employable white males will decline. Thus, morality and altruism (and even law) pale as driving forces for equity when compared to the imperative of American economic survival. There will be no prosperity if our workplaces and educational institutions do not respond aggressively to demographic trends. Change must occur in both the workforce make-up and climate. Our economic base and our social and educational institutional frameworks will depend on the education, income, and support of many who are not now included or utilized according to their numbers or potential (i.e., people of color, women, the differently abled, gays, lesbians).

Institutions of higher education and their academic libraries are both affected by, and have a special responsibility for, helping society meet its economic imperative. Higher education must prepare all citizens, including the now white majority, to live in a multicultural, pluralistic society and to be sensitive to issues of gender and alternative life-styles. In addition, people of color and women must be educated in greater numbers for positions in all areas of the economy. To do this, the demographic composition of the faculty and staff, as well as the student body, will have to change, as will the curricula and support structures now in place.

The academic library is and will be a key unit in affecting change in the academy. Second only to the faculty in standing for knowledge and the pursuit of truth, the library is highly visible and essential to the teaching and research process. As the point of intersection, the physical and intellectual meeting place for all segments of the community, the library has a special relationship with faculty, administration, and students. Its collections legitimize and identify areas worthy of scholarship. To effectively serve the educational and research needs of a changing faculty and student body, the library will have to reexamine and change its own mix of staff, collections, services, and physical facilities. The key to success will be a diversified workforce committed to a pluralistic philosophy and sensitive to the positive value of differences. Without a diversified workforce, other changes will not be effective or sustained. As the library undertakes this change, it can serve as a model and provide support for other efforts in the institution.

Given the past failures to achieve a society where diverse individuals thrive, can organizations and libraries actually achieve this goal? What have past efforts taught us? One clear lesson is that individuals and individual attitudes do matter. People act on their beliefs and attitudes. Their paradigms (or internal information processes) determine how new information will be received and acted upon, and thus, decide which beliefs and attitudes should change. Until individuals understand how their beliefs and paradigms may militate against equity and diversity, lasting fundamental change is impossible.

Every individual must accept responsibility for creating an equitable, diverse society and must act on this responsibility daily. The formal structure—laws and rules governing society and the workplace—remains important and requires constant refinement by senior administrators and managers. However, rules, laws and procedures are not enough.

Organizations must be fundamentally rethought. Our organizations are not neutral; their structure revolves around the culture, values, and rules of the dominant white heterosexual male society. In such an environment, treating people the same does not equal treating them equitably nor does it ensure that talent and hard work, regardless of color, gender, or sexual orientation, are the ultimate keys to success. Focusing equity efforts on sameness and color blindness misjudges how greatly self-esteem, confidence, and security are rooted in racial, sexual, and cultural identities. Ignoring race, gender, sexual orientation, or other differences ignores basic personality aspects. It essentially says to persons of color, women, gays or lesbians that they must overcome their handicap and become like white, heterosexual males to succeed. It denies the positive value of difference, as well as the opportunity for those possessing that difference to thrive, contribute, and strengthen the organization.

The charge that affirmative action and hiring goals or targets are unique entitlement programs that constitute reverse discrimination is a myth. The myth stems from the belief that there have been no inherent advantages, privileges, or entitlement programs for whites in education or the workplace. However, white privilege does exist.[2] Entitlement programs have always existed for whites and are taken for granted. For example, in colleges and universities, the practice of preferential acceptance for children of alumni acts as an entitlement primarily enjoyed by white males. This entitlement has had a larger economic impact than all affirmative action programs to date. Furthermore, the current, most frequently used qualification criteria for filling positions in education and the workplace are those developed by white males for white males. Their bias leans toward formal higher education. The current mentoring and human resource development practices and programs in most organizations also reflect similar white male entitlements, having been developed specifically to prepare white males for the next step on the career ladder. They center on male activities and male social interaction patterns. Yet, these entitlements or advantages have not been seen as unequal, nor are those who use them stigmatized for discriminating. Quite the contrary, they generally benefit the individuals in both society and the workplace.

All of the foregoing, plus the day-to-day unconscious misuse of language perpetuates a hostile climate—e.g., pairing the word "qualified" with "women and minorities" in recruitment advertisements implies that most are not or that men are assumed to be automatically qualified. Women and minorities daily deal with verbal and nonverbal slights, including ethnic and racial jokes and averted eye contact by whites to avoid acknowledging their presence. The expectation that workplace newcomers lose their racial or sexual identity to become white male in behavior and attitude makes most organizations hostile, not positive or even neutral, environments. Thus, the environments themselves hinder the creation and nurturing of a diversified workforce and militate against the positive contributions of such a workforce. The University of Michigan Library has learned that environments and organizational climates are important for success.

How do organizations use and build upon what has been learned to create and sustain a diversified workforce? First, senior administrators must define what is meant by diversity and must clearly establish the goal of diversifying. Diversity is a social construct, not a legal one. It signifies an acceptance of difference and represents an attempt to speak to the positive value of having individuals of different backgrounds, race, gender, physical skills, or sexual orientation in the organization. It represents a commitment to move from preserving dominant white, European male perspectives and values to accepting, recognizing, and encouraging new values and perspectives that can be brought only by individuals with significant life experiences outside the dominant culture. Diversity does *not* mean a melting pot, a newly homogenous culture. It means thriving difference. By diversifying, the organization becomes a better place for members of the dominant culture as well as others. By diversifying, the organization unleashes creative forces that will make it more effective in the long run. The bottom line for diversity is to make the organization more productive in fulfilling its mission.

A diversified workforce cannot be sustained and nurtured unless an organization, in this case a library, becomes multicultural:

- Reflects the contributions and interests of diverse cultural and social groups in its mission, operations and product or service.
- Acts on a commitment to the eradication of social oppression in all forms in the organization. It is also sensitive to the possible violation of the interests of all cultural and social groups whether or not they are represented in the organization.
- [Has] members of diverse cultural and social groups [who] are full participants at all levels of the organization, especially in those areas where decisions are made that shape the organization.
- Follows through on its broader social responsibilities including its support of efforts to eliminate all forms of social oppression. This also involves the support of efforts to expand the multicultural ideology.[3]

A multicultural organization understands that each person makes a unique and positive contribution to society and does so because, not in spite, of his or her differences. A multicultural organization, therefore, looks for differences in each new hire. Affirmative action goals or targets set minimums, not maximums. Recruitment is aggressive, continually seeking new methods and sources for identifying talented individuals, continually reviewing job criteria and qualifications to ensure the stated abilities and skills pertain only to those necessary to actually do the job. People of difference need *not* be overqualified or superstars to be hired. The myths are as follows:

1. There aren't "any" out there,
2. Any non-white hire is not qualified, or is less qualified than white candidates, and
3. White males are discriminated against in hiring or promotion when people of difference are hired are debunked. They are exposed as the tired excuses they are for not achieving diversity.

In the multicultural organization, training and intern programs exist to increase the numbers of potential candidates in the pipeline and are seen as "fair" and necessary entitlement programs. Regular "climate checks" ensure that people of color or other differences are not isolated in one part of the organization or relegated to certain jobs or pay ranges. A multicultural organization monitors performance evaluation systems and merit rankings for conscious or unconscious bias. It questions differential attrition rates. It focuses on trends, not individual cases or excuses for a person of difference's departure or dismissal. It regularly trains supervisors in the necessary skills to manage and nurture a diversified workforce. Barriers to promotion—plateaus or glass ceilings for people of color and women—are systematically identified and eradicated. A multicultural organization does not expect people of difference to identify barriers or educate their colleagues as to problems or acceptable behavior. It questions its own language and makes sensitivity everyone's business. Difference is valued, utilized, and promoted.

Bailey Jackson and Evangelina Holvino at the Center for Research on Social Organization created a useful model for developing a multicultural organization.[4] The model is divided into six stages within three levels:

LEVEL I: THE MONOCULTURAL ORGANIZATION

This level seeks to maintain the status quo by "enhancing the dominance, privilege, and access of those in power."

Stage 1

The Exclusionary Organization is primarily interested in the dominance of one group over other oppressed groups on the basis of sex, race, gender, or cultural identity.

Stage 2

The *Club* does not outwardly espouse white male supremacy but does act out views in an attempt to maintain control and privileges of those who have traditionally held power.

LEVEL II: THE NON-DISCRIMINATING ORGANIZATION

This level consists of "non discrimination in a monocultural context"—i.e., it admits people of different cultures into the organization without changing fundamentally.

Stage 3

The Compliance Organization is committed to removing some of the discrimination found in the earlier stage of the Club by allowing minorities and women to enter, but avoids tampering with the actual structure, mission, and culture of the organization in the process. The organization's method for changing the racial and gender profile is often to actively recruit and hire more racial minorities and women at the bottom of the system. If they are hired or promoted into management positions, they are generally seen as "tokens," and must be "qualified team players." They must be exceptional and not openly challenge the organization's mission and practices.

Stage 4

The Affirmative Action Organization actively recruits and promotes women, racial minorities, and members of other social groups which are generally denied access. Moreover, support of the growth and development of these minority employees is demonstrated through programs that increase their chances of success and mobility in the organization. The Affirmative Action Organization has evolved and now addresses employee attitudes toward oppression, conducts workshops on racial and sexual discrimination, and broadens its perception of diversity to include all socially oppressed groups. Regardless of this, the organization members remain committed to conforming to the norms and practices of the majority group's world view.

LEVEL III: THE MULTICULTURAL ORGANIZATION

This level emphasizes: "a) diverse cultural representation; b) equitable distribution of power and influence; c) the elimination of oppression; and d) multicultural perspectives in the larger society."

Stage 5

The Redefining Organization. No longer content with just being anti-racist or anti-sexist, a commitment is made to examine the organization's activities for their impact on all of its members' ability to participate in and to contribute to the organization's growth and success. The limitations of the prevailing cultural perspective are questioned as to their influences on the organization's mission, structure, management, technology, psychosocial dynamics, and product or service. New approaches and alternative methods of organizing are explored which guarantee the inclusion, participation, and empowerment of all of the organization's members.

Stage 6

The Multicultural Organization. The creation of a multicultural organization is a process that will take a long time. No organization has achieved the status of a true multicultural organization. There is no overnight fix. Change efforts must be systematic, comprehensive, multi-faceted, multi-interventionist, and multi-year. There is no checklist of right things to do or series of events, which once held, will lead to success. It is more difficult to manage a diversified workforce, because it includes different people with *legitimate* different wants and ideas on what and how work should be done. The path will not be smooth and mistakes will be made. However, progress can be made in the short run if

mistakes are acknowledged and learned from and it is regularly stressed that managing diversity is challenging new work.
The key element for creating a multicultural organization is
accepting that it is a *process*, not a product. New issues will constantly emerge as old ones are resolved. The work is never done.
Senior administration must set the tone, give direction, and
define the goals as an organization moves toward multiculturalism. They must create forums and opportunities for people to
examine their own attitudes and beliefs and become open to
differences. Formal and informal rules for acceptable organizational behavior must be established which clearly define the
boundaries. Pressure must be created, people made uncomfortable, resources allocated or reallocated, and support and education provided.

Multiculturalism and diversity efforts must be constantly
brought to the attention of organizational members. They must
be frequently raised in management discussions. The organization must be constantly monitored and actions and results,
not intent, measured. Outside help and research must be
sought and applied. A broad-based sense of ownership among
individuals in the organization must be created. There must
be support networks to help prevent burn-out among those
most actively involved. Middle level management must be involved, prepared, and supported in diversity and multicultural efforts.

The process of creating a multicultural organization begins with individual education. Individuals must understand
and deal with their own unconscious discriminatory attitudes
and behaviors. Managers must create a safe environment to
encourage such exploration. Backlash must be expected, accepted and seen as a positive sign of progress, not a signal to stop,
or slow down.

Managers must also develop effective methods for han-
dling human resource related issues in a multicultural organization and an ability to interpret workplace dynamics that are
influenced by racism, sexism, homophobia, etc. They must
overcome their own management limitations based on:

1. their lack of consideration of any other cultural perspective other than the dominant white perspective as the
   right way to do business,
2. their lack of consideration for the impact that racial/cul-
   tural difference is going to have on the way that workplace issues and tools are approached, and

3. their lack of consideration for the impact that racism and sexism have on the workforce, especially a diverse workforce.

An inherent consequence of diversifying the racial profile of an organization is heightened concerns and awareness of diversity. Therefore, managers must have the ability to expand their understanding of diversity (race, sex, sexual orientation) as a significant variable in human development and interaction. Managers must be able to recognize when and how racism and sexism affect their own perspective and that of other members of the organization.[5]

Managers must recognize and confront the tendency to focus on the weaknesses or deficiencies of employees and applicants of difference, rather than on the strengths they bring as is done with white males. Managers can develop the necessary understandings for managing a diversified workforce by making use of readily available research and applicable models. For instance, the racial identity development model proposed by Bailey Jackson and Rita Hardiman describes the consciousness of Blacks and Whites as they move through the developmental process and the implications that their consciousness has for the way they view themselves and the way they view and interact with their environment.[6]

Institutions and senior management should expect no gratitude or positive recognition for moving toward a multicultural organization. For people of difference and those committed to a multicultural organization, changes are long overdue. For those who have not yet accepted the multicultural goal, a little diversity goes a long way. From them, management is likely to hear "What is enough?" "Isn't this going overboard?" "Hasn't our affirmative action goal been reached?" Senior management must remember that the change to multiculturalism is not the result of altruism or the desire to do the right thing for individuals, although these would be good enough reasons. It is a necessary response to the economic survival imperative.

Libraries are not responsible for the monoculturalism that pervades American society, including the academy. However, libraries do not exist in a vacuum isolated from society or the general campus. Libraries are accountable for their response to their own and the institution's efforts. For society to maintain a competitive economic base, the academy must prepare a diversity of individuals for effective participation in society. The academy must equip the next generation of leaders, white males and people of difference, to live and work together effectively. The academy itself will not survive as a vital social institution if it does not succeed at those tasks. The library has a special role and a unique responsibility to help the academy with these tasks. Libraries are points of intersection—the crossroads for people and ideas. The library must be a place where individuals can make the most of their educational opportunities and at the same time learn about diversity. To offer diversity, libraries must become diversified. They must become multicultural organizations, they must develop multicultural knowledge bases, and they must provide leadership for the rest of the campus and academic community.

REFERENCES

1. Commission on Minority Participation in Education and American Life, *One-third of a Nation: A Report of the Commission on Minority Participation in Education and American Life* (Washington, D.C.: American Council on Education; Denver, CO: Education Commission of the States, 1988), p. 35.
2. Peggy McIntosh, "White Privilege: Unpacking the Invisible Knapsack," *Peace and Freedom*, 49 (1989), p. 10.
3. Ibid.
4. Bailey Jackson and Evangelina Holvino, *Multicultural Organization Development,* Center for Research on Social Organization. (Working Paper no. 356, 1982), pp. 4-8.
5. Bailey Jackson and Rita Hardiman, "Racial Identity Development," *Implications for Managing the Multicultural Workforce* (Unpublished paper, 1982), p. 12.
6. Ibid.

3

Top Management's Commitment and Role

Donald E. Riggs

In general, libraries do not have a commendable track record in cultural diversity. This inadequate performance may stem from top library management's failure to recognize and act upon the importance of integrating cultural diversity endeavors. While several success stories of more people of color employed in libraries can be told, many libraries' efforts in cultural diversity stop with the personnel component, neglecting the significance of collections, services, and other supplemental dimensions.

The expansion of diversity activities in all types of libraries is an encouraging sign that top management is beginning to understand the impact of cultural diversity on the entire construct of the library. Without solid management commitment for these activities, they will likely fail. Leading-edge libraries declare commitment to the value of diversity; top management of these libraries walk the talk of diversity when setting goals and policies. They speak the language of diversity, and are motivated learners in seeking additional knowledge about diversity issues. Top management in this chapter refers to deans, directors, and university librarians.

LINKING DIVERSITY TO STRATEGIC VISION

In recent years, libraries have used strategic planning in creating blueprints for the future. For the library's diversity program to have credibility, it is critical to link diversity with the library's long-range strategic vision. A library-wide diversity program affects the various goals and objectives of all library divisions, departments, and units. The strategic vision focuses on the changes expected to library personnel, collections, and services, and concentrates on the interactive, pluralistic aspects of areas throughout the library. In other words, no one dimension of the library functions as an isolated part of the diversity endeavor. Ideally, a library's strategic vision conforms with its parent institution's strategic vision. However, even if the parent institution lacks a strategic vision, the library must formulate its own. When visualizing future diversity pursuits, the library staff should perceive new realities and develop a sense of shared purpose. The diverse needs and expectations of the library users should guide the creation of the strategic vision. The articulation of a pluralistic vision should denote many long-term advantages for the library and its users.

Long-Range and Annual Planning

With an established strategic vision, library management must develop a three- to five-year strategic plan. Planning experts discourage attempts to write 10- to 15-year plans. The three- to five-year plan remains focused when updated annually and implemented through an annual working plan. Even though the library's top managers initiate and lead the planning endeavor, the planning activities should eventually result from a "bottom-up" process. Cultural diversity emphases must be reflected throughout the plan. For example, plans for new facilities must include accommodations for the disabled user.

The word "diversity" should be included in the library's mission statement. The mission statement—the grand abstract design for the library—supports the long-range strategic vision. Following the mission statement, a strategic plan articulates the long-range goals. Long-range plans for libraries typically specify goals for improving recruiting and retention of minorities without incorporating multiculturalism in all the various goals. Goals must be written in clear and operational terms. Participation by library staff in goal-setting serves as the best motivator for realizing the goals.

With goals developed, attention turns to the objectives. Written in specific terms, objectives are short-term, purposeful, measurable, and consistent with goals. Objectives plot the specific course for achieving each goal by defining the library's intentions and ranking the priority for each step. The library's cultural diversity committee must take an active role in the development of the mission statement, goals, and objectives.

Finally, the plan formulates program strategies. Strategies reduce goals and objectives to a concrete, detailed level. Normally carefully conceived and well-planned, they sometimes emerge from ad hoc circumstances as well. Even though the cultural diversity committee plays a role in the other components of the planning process, its most important task lies in the formulation of strategies. Strategies form the core of strategic planning. Top management must assume responsibility for making strategies consistent, appropriate in view of resources, acceptable in degree of risk, and achievable within an appropriate timeline.

The long-range strategic plan drives the annual library plan. Annual plans, or yearly business plans, delineate goals and objectives for a given year and focus the activity during the course of the year. Working with an annual plan, one observes more immediate results in diversity. However, the emphasis should not neglect the long term. Immediate results provide evidence that management takes diversity seriously, but long-term commitment to an on-going process is of greater value to the diversity program and the library.

The Evaluation Process

Every planning activity should have an evaluation process, asking questions like "What went right?" and "What went wrong?" Careful review of the diversity strategies determines whether the respective strategies should be maintained for the next year, merged with another strategy, or eliminated. Diversity strategies can be evaluated in the same manner as most other strategies in areas of collections, services, and personnel. Strategy formulation and implementation requires a strong human dimension if expected results are to be gleaned; the library staff is and will continue to be the most precious resource. Fairness, honesty, and forthrightness are important ingredients in the recipe for strategy formulation.

"INSTITUTIONALIZING" DIVERSITY THROUGHOUT THE LIBRARY

Top management alone can not achieve diversity. For diversity to become truly effective throughout the library, everyone must genuinely engage in the endeavor. Many service organizations, including libraries, merely react to the diversity movement. Some remain passive, believing diversity to be a fad that will pass. But diversity will not go away. Libraries that remain inert and silent on diversity issues skate on thinner and thinner ice. Quick fixes only temporarily solve problems; incorporating diversity in the library's strategic planning process is crucial. Diversity is a long-term endeavor, one of the more difficult challenges ever facing libraries. Users, for example, demand services not currently offered. The confusion, swirling rhetoric, and lack of common understanding must cease. Library administrators must exercise leadership in defining clearly what diversity means and how its intentions and purposes will be delivered. These administrators must become proactionary and develop a "diversity philosophy." This philosophy articulates how we make diversity effective library-wide. We cannot be effective change agents unless our philosophy and action mesh.

WHO SETS THE TEMPO FOR MULTICULTURALISM

The library director (dean, university librarian, head librarian) is the person in the library who can and should set the tempo for multiculturalism. The concept of diversity should become a way of life in the library; it cannot be perceived as a trend or fad. If the director has only a luke-warm attitude toward diversity and there are no apparent signs of change, it is only a matter of time before diversity efforts fade. The director must believe in and project unwavering commitment to multiculturalism, must speak and write about the importance of valuing commonalities and dissimilarities. Various interests and backgrounds must be acknowledged, legitimized, understood, and—as a long-term goal—appreciated. Aspiring to become a multicultural library keeps racial and ethnic differences at the forefront. Results-oriented directors serve as leaders, not observers, in advancing diversity.

The Role of the Associate and Assistant Director

The associate and assistant directors also play an important role in articulating a pluralistic vision. By the nature of their place in the library's hierarchy, they should share the director's perspective of diversity and must pursue the established library-wide goals and objectives. We cannot tell others to do what we say if we do not do it ourselves. If the library has a deputy director, this officer can further refine the director's diversity aspirations. For example, while Carla Stoffle served as Deputy Director of the University of Michigan Library, she provided the extra push required for promoting diversity in the library. Due largely to her efforts, the University of Michigan Library received the University's first Affirmative Action Award and was recognized as a Model Diversity Program on campus. As divisional strategic plans often offer innovative strategies, associate and assistant directors should develop strategic plans that tie-in with and support the library-wide plan.

The divisional strategic planning process permits a bit of entrepreneurship, but risk-taking should be limited to calculated risk. One should not, for example, over-commit the division's budget for diversity or any other activity. The associate and assistant directors can serve as role models by discussing their awareness development and their efforts to manage personal stereotypes and prejudices, as well as by simply displaying the day-to-day behaviors required to lead and inspire the division. These managers must possess skills for resolving culture clashes between and among diverse work groups. Collectively, the associate and assistant directors create the organizational structure that spreads the library-wide vision between and among the various divisions, and increases commitment among diverse employees at all organizational levels. Diversity pursuits must not be narrowly prescribed for only a few library departments or units.

The Role of the Department Head

As an often overlooked library administrator, the department head receives little attention in library literature. Although generally not perceived as a member of the library's top management, department heads serve as the linchpin between the majority of library employees and top management. Operating closer to the moment-of-truth work level, they understand staff and user expectations of the staff and users better than those in the top echelons. Without the enthusiastic support of department heads, the library's diversity activities stagnate. Department heads take an important leadership role by building diversity into their departmental strategic plans and by integrating diversity goals with their staff's annual goals.

At the University of Michigan Library, the Dean of the University Library asks assistant directors to include diversity goals in annual department goals. Some department heads take this practice to the next step (i.e., including diversity goals in respective staff's annual goals). The commitment to diversity goes beyond the library's top management. All library administrators and their respective staff should make the commitment.

Like several other libraries, the University of Michigan Library created a diversity librarian position and, like others, still refines the position. Presently, Michigan's diversity librarian reports to the head of the Graduate Library. This reporting structure appears to work well, but may require alteration to develop the position's perception as a library-wide position. Michigan's Undergraduate Library also assigns a person to work with diversity issues and sit on the library's diversity committee. The library's top management supports both positions, although the hierarchy in which the diversity librarian reports to someone other than the library director may suggest faint commitment for library-wide diversity by top management. But it should not. Some diversity librarians were employed with the understanding that they would have limited responsibilities. As the position of diversity librarian matures and widens during the next few years, specific responsibilities will become better understood and delineated. Creating this important position, even in times of limited financial means, solidly exhibits top management's firm support of the multicultural effort. In 1993 the University of Michigan Library created a new position, Assistant to the Dean for Cultural Diversity; this position is responsible for cultural diversity leadership librarywide.

To work effectively together in the library, all employees need a common sense of purpose and a shared commitment to the library's goals. Diversity will not become institutionalized with a casual, disjointed approach. In the past, creating the united sense of purpose required getting others to accept the values and perspectives of the dominant group. Today, the task is more complicated. In the University of Michigan Library, we are making substantial progress toward a shared sense of purpose. Instead of imposing mainstream values on others, our library is beginning to recognize the importance of building a solid foundation of shared values. A "buy-in" is occurring within our diverse work force. With a gradual assimilation and integration of shared values, diversity is indeed becoming institutionalized in our library.

FROM TRANSACTIONAL
TO TRANSFORMATIONAL LEADERSHIP

For libraries to become more than affirmative action institutions, strong leadership is required. Diversity has a more complex and compelling thrust than affirmative action. It demands a change in leadership behavior. Too many times, library leaders are transactional when they should be transformational. A transactional leader reacts to issues on a day-to-day basis, seldom taking risks. The transformational leader takes the initiative in creating new approaches to old problems, implements changes readily, makes (instead of waits for) things happen, and uses entrepreneurial skills. Institutionalizing diversity requires transformational leaders, leaders who enjoy inventing the future, who acutely understand the urgency for making library-wide diversity a reality. Richard Dougherty and Robert Warner, both former directors of the University of Michigan Library, demonstrated transformational leadership in their development and nurturing of the diversity program; credit for beginning the multicultural perspective currently perpetuated in the UM Library belongs to them. Even though the UM Library has made a fine start in developing an infrastructure for diversity, much work remains. This library-wide effort challenges the imagination and entrepreneurship of the library's top managers. Creative approaches set a climate encouraging change, promote collaborative alliances among the library's diverse staff, and get fast results. The majority of the library's staff maintains and supports the core principles guiding diversity. Transforming leaders sustains the philosophy of valuing diversity as a top agenda item and provides evidence of solid progression toward enhancing this philosophy and its implications.

IMPROVING COMMUNICATION

The library's diversity philosophy must be conveyed as often as possible. Communication minimizes fear, frustration, and misapprehension. The lack of communication, rather than an excess of it, concerns all of us interested in promoting a better understanding of our intentions and purposes. The responsibility for enhancing two-way communication rests with the library's top management.

Including diversity in the various components of the library's strategic plan sends a strong message about the top management's commitment to diversity. At the University of Michigan Library, the Dean of University Library devotes entire sessions of the Dean's Assembly (including all library department heads and other key administrators) meetings to diversity. These sessions allow the Dean and the cultural diversity committee to inform library administrators about the committee and top management's past activities and future ideas. These mutually beneficial meetings recognize that differences between primary and secondary dimensions of diversity often produce differences in the way messages are sent and received. Rules of effective communication increase in importance and complexity as diversity expands, and the rules for effective cross-cultural communication continue to evolve.

Along with topical meetings, cultural diversity can be communicated with the library staff via the library newsletter, written and oral communiques from the director, special diversity programs, bulletin boards and exhibits, and other appropriate modes of interaction.

In addition to using effective communication mechanisms, library management must be cognizant of socio-cultural effects on communication, how different methods and styles of communication can convey the same message. As the University of Michigan Library has witnessed, failure to appreciate how communication styles differ leaves only the lens of our own socialization through which to evaluate others' messages. Until we recognize subtle differences in the communication styles of our library colleagues, we will expect them to behave exactly as we do. We must recognize key variables in communication to more aptly gauge the impact of style on others. Since nearly all communication involves a transmitter and a receiver, library managers, in particular, must learn to listen effectively. Listening is a dimension of communication that is often misunderstood and undervalued. Communication is one of the more complex aspects of managing a diverse work force. One must understand and practice the differences in style, be aware of language sensitivities, and adhere to a lexicon of appropriate terms.

BUDGETING

Some perceive the budget as the best place for library managers to show their commitment to diversity. Money is undoubtedly important; action normally entails resources. However, budgeting must follow the diversity philosophy. Regardless of the library's financial resources, a genuine belief in and understanding of the importance of diversity forms the essential cornerstone.

Diverse personnel is basic for a multicultural library and may warrant a redeployment of funds to proactively achieve. Money can be the leverage tool needed to create an environment reflective of society's multicultural character. In addition to fruitful recruitment from diverse racial and ethnic groups, we must aggressively identify local talent and give diverse library staff an opportunity to gain the M.L.S. or other appropriate degrees. Initiating local talent into the mainstream library, providing them with credentials and experience, should be high on the agenda of library management. Funds will have to be found or re-allocated to support diversity programs, workshops, institutes, and other continuing education activities. Library managers cannot boast of active or strong multiculturalism without making provisions for the growth and development of minorities before external forces mandate internal change.

The managers responsible for developing the library's collections must constantly remain aware of the need to make available information resources that support instruction and research from a pluralistic perspective. In addition to major trade publications, libraries should purchase primary source documents pertaining to ethnicity, race, and sexual orientation. Censorship toward any group must not be tolerated. Bibliographic access must improve to better serve the users of diverse collections. Empirical data must replace the former practice of relying on perceptions in determining collection adequacy. In 1991, a gay and lesbian task force at the University of Michigan developed a list of recommended resources and, fortunately, found the UM Library to have an adequate collection of gay and lesbian information.

The multicultural library contains many diverse services for its users. Outreach programs such as one administered by the UM Undergraduate Library often successfully meet their goals and objectives. Disabled users deserve greater attention at the University of Michigan and elsewhere. New funds or re-allocated resources will have to be found for these services. Diversity may call for more funding, but money should follow the enactment of a sound philosophy, not vice versa. Doing the right thing has a price, but continuing to do what is wrong costs more.

TOTAL QUALITY MANAGEMENT

Many organizations, including libraries, now use the principles of Total Quality Management (TQM). When the University of Michigan decided to use TQM, its library actively engaged in quality improvement. Philip Crosby, Edwards Deming, and Joseph Juran are the three TQM gurus recognized in the management literature. Deming became renown for his work with the Japanese in quality improvement—dating back to the 1950s. All three agree that to have a TQM program an organization must

1. Have a *total* commitment to quality,
2. Be customer (user) driven,
3. Eliminate rework,
4. Place emphasis on teamwork,
5. Give high priority to training,
6. Respect and empower all people in the organization, and
7. Create an ongoing appreciation for quality.

TQM places a high premium on quality, making the library a natural location for implementing this management technique. The high priority given to training, teamwork, and empowering and respecting people fits perfectly with the library's cultural diversity activities. Moreover, as TQM meshes with the library's management, it forces managers to be more cognizant of multiculturalism. TQM depends largely on carefully crafted plans that can be realized by systematic implementation. Improved products and services benefit users—a basic goal of all library managers. The training component of TQM benefits all library employees, whatever their ethnicity. TQM training programs encourage the creativity and innovative potential of each library employee. TQM also exponentially complements the diversity endeavor with its emphasis on the empowerment of and respect for all library staff members.

Empowering and Respecting People

TQM advocates changing the culture of the library. A metamorphosis comes primarily from the emphasis placed on empowering and respecting the entire library staff. Based on observations in the business world, TQM emphatically fulfills both goals. TQM proponents trace most organization problems to its processes, not its people. They believe administrators should stop attacking people and look more critically at the processes and systems. People generally want to do the right thing and want to take pride in their work. A logical and humane approach to problem solving gives the library staff who actually do the work the power and opportunity to change improper or ineffective ways of operating. Invisible walls between the professional and non-professional staff disappear when the library develops strategic teams. Self-respect increases when an empowered staff garners more credit and satisfaction from doing quality work. If every member of the library staff, regardless of status or ethnicity, race, or sexual orientation, should gain more empowerment and greater respect, TQM and cultural diversity make an excellent match. The impact TQM has on diversity depends upon the matchmaker—i.e., top management.

MENTORING AND INTERNSHIPS

Library management has a timely leadership opportunity in fostering mentoring programs and internships. Both activities benefit the diversity efforts immensely. Several library directors believe a mentor helped shape their careers. Some even report that the mentoring they received was the most important factor in their careers. Top library management, in particular, plays an important role in the development of professional minority staff; mentoring a minority librarian interested in becoming a library manager can be done easily and informally.

Library managers can create internship opportunities for new and mid-career library staff. This effort especially steps in the right direction for people of color interested in working with experienced professionals. Internships must be carefully designed for the intern to have a meaningful experience; the intern should be challenged, given experience of significant value that results in a demonstrable expertise.

Mentoring programs and internships must never be designed or implemented in a manner causing perceptions that ghettoize ethnic staff into minority-type positions. Good intentions can do more harm than good to the diversity effort if not implemented judiciously.

CONCLUSION

Library managers can lend valuable assistance in the creation of diversity programs. Lack of funding does not excuse failure to diversify. Transformational leadership, coupled with strategic vision, inspires the necessary climate for striving to become a multicultural library. Through modern management techniques such as strategic planning and total quality management, a systematic and dynamic approach unfolds once commitment has taken hold. All levels of library personnel, all levels of service, and all aspects of the collections should be considered in the diversity effort. Top management must go beyond a one-dimensional approach to the diversity challenge if it expects to have a genuine, comprehensive endeavor. It must understand that diversity is multifaceted, and management's philosophy and practice should reflect a shared sense of purpose that extends throughout the library.

Sometimes choices must be made between doing the right things and doing things right. A successful diversity program continually refines itself to accomplish both simultaneously. Nevertheless, responsible library managers cannot abdicate their leadership role in seeking to do the right things. Strong commitment to diversity does not include any short cuts or half measures. Triggers for positive changes in the library's philosophy on diversity can only be pulled by dedicated library managers. With nearly everything in a state of flux, these managers no longer alter events in a fixed context. The contemporary library manager must understand reality well enough to replace the former cookie-cutter approach with one that views diversity as a vital and varying element. As we move into the next millennium, diversity will provide an extraordinary challenge for library managers. It is high time to make preparations to deal effectively with this momentous opportunity.

4

The Myths
and Realities
of Affirmative Action

Zaida I. Giraldo

The term "affirmative action," indicating some activity beyond the neutral stance of non-discrimination, was first used in Executive Order 10925 issued by President Kennedy on March 6, 1961. Prior to that date, all governmental policies dealt solely with non-discrimination in employment and mainly limited themselves to merely outlawing various forms of discrimination in federal employment. The prohibition against discrimination on account of religion was the first to appear in the Civil Service Act of 1883. In 1933, when Congress adopted the Unemployment Relief Act, it identified other forms of discrimination, namely race and color, in addition to the by-then established prohibition against religious discrimination. This act appropriated federal dollars for persons left unemployed by the private sector and extended the non-discrimination protection provided to federal employees to these persons. In Executive Order 8587 issued by President Roosevelt in 1940, race, color, and religion became protected categories in regard to non-discrimination in employment by federal contractors, thereby extending federal employment rules to the private sector. Such an extension was allowed because the existence of a signed contract between the parties enabled the imposition of terms agreeable to both parties. If a contractor wanted to do business with the federal government, it had to promise not to discriminate on account of race, color, or religion in its hiring policies for its own employees.

All of this governmental protective activity, however, represented expressions of policy with no follow through. No machinery was established to investigate whether the government or the federal contractors actually implemented these policies or to ensure their enforcement. This changed on June 25, 1941 when President Roosevelt established the first Fair Employment Practices Committee (FEPC) as an independent agency responsible to him. Its responsibility was

> To encourage full participation in the national defense program by all citizens of the United States, regardless of race, creed, color, or national origin in the firm belief that the democratic way of life within the nation can be defended successfully only with the help and support of all groups within its borders.[1]

Unfortunately, the inherent weakness of the FEPC, due to its small size and budget in comparison to its broad mandate, caused it to dissolve early in 1943. However, as World War II was still being fought, and the need for every available worker no matter what color, race, religion, or the newly added category of national origin grew, a replacement FEPC was established by President Roosevelt in 1943. This new committee had the power to monitor all federal contracts, not just those held by companies doing defense work, and received sufficient funds to establish 15 field offices and eventually process approximately 8,000 discrimination complaints. It never had the power to enforce its decisions, however, and discontinued its work in 1946 soon after the end of the war. Under President Truman, Executive Order 10308 created an 11 member replacement committee to monitor government contractors, and was expanded to a 15 member group under President Eisenhower. Neither committee, however, showed the energy of the war time committee in the execution of its anti-discrimination mandate.

All of this federal activity could be characterized as efforts to establish the principles of equal opportunity and non-discrimination which are, in fact, very passive concepts. The only promise made was that an employer would *not* discriminate in future employment decisions. The employer had no obligation to do anything about the discrimination which might have occurred prior to the passage of the act. No remedy was applied to the legacy of the past: the enormous social and economic inequities brought about by hundreds of years of discrimination and de jure and de facto segregation. This approach finally changed when President Kennedy added the two words "affirmative action" to his executive order in 1961. Those two words, by themselves, sent the signal that government would take responsibility for going beyond pious statements of principle promising only prospective relief to taking steps to redress the legacy of discrimination.

Executive Order 10925

The affirmative action program envisioned in Executive Order 10925 was a very modest one. It required that federal contractors state their commitment to treat all applicants without regard to race, creed, color or national origin in all solicitations or advertisements for workers. More importantly, it required contractors to advise the labor unions with which they dealt of their commitment to non-discrimination and to extend their obligation under the order to their unions and subcontractors. It also obligated contractors to follow the regulations issued by the newly established Commission on Equal Employment Opportunity and to comply with any investigation initiated by that group. Finally, and probably most importantly in terms of the long run, it required the filing of regular compliance reports so that the hiring and employment practices of federal contractors could be monitored.

The enforcement provisions of the Kennedy Executive Order had teeth. It authorized the publication of the names of noncomplying contractors and the termination of the rights of such contractors to do business with the federal government. It also allowed Justice Department prosecution to compel compliance with the contract provisions and forbade agencies to enter into new contracts with contractors found in violation of their previous contracts. The commission was very active and, in a little over two years, had signed "plans for progress" with over 200 contractors, describing the enhanced efforts these firms would make to attract members of minority groups to available employment opportunities. In June 1963, President Kennedy signed Executive Order 1114, extending the coverage of E.O. 10925 to all federal construction contractors and to construction firms using federal loans or credit, as well as to firms relying on federal grants, loans, insurance, or guarantees.

Executive Order 11246

In September 1965, President Johnson issued what has become the fundamental document in affirmative action, namely Executive Order 11246 which superseded E.O. 10925 and E.O. 1114. This order again prohibited discrimination on the basis of race, creed, color and national origin by federal contractors, but also established the Department of Labor as the agency responsible for ensuring compliance. In October of that year Willard Wirtz, then Secretary of Labor, established the Office of Federal Contract Compliance, later the Office of Federal Contract Compliance Programs (OFCCP), to regulate and monitor compliance with the Executive Order. The original Executive Order required affirmative action for minorities, but in 1968 the order was amended, and the OFCCP also became responsible for affirmative action on behalf of women who had been excluded from many traditionally-male occupations.

When the OFCCP issued Revised Order #4 in 1972, the fundamental rules for affirmative action were laid down by the federal government. Affirmative action, as defined by these rules, required all federal contractors to take steps to recruit members of protected groups and to treat them fairly once employed. In addition, certain contractors holding contracts of $50,000 and above became required to draw up annual affirmative action plans (AAP). The AAP required the announcement and dissemination of an equal opportunity and affirmative action policy by the head of the firm, along with the establishment of a number of technical procedures to allow for the measurement of progress in the area of affirmative action. Revised Order

#4 introduced the concept of setting goals to achieve a representative workforce. The concept of goal-setting was based on the belief that affirmative action meant eliminating historic patterns of discrimination from the labor force. To change those patterns, a system for identifying the patterns and for setting annual goals to change the patterns had to be designed.

GOALS ESTABLISHED BY THE OFCCP

The goal setting system established by the OFCCP was deceptively simple. The system required each federal contractor to break down its workforce into job groups and to compare their representation of minorities and women with the representation found in the relevant labor force: the national, regional, state, or local labor pool—whichever was relevant in terms of a reasonable recruitment area depending on the type of job. A national labor pool was used if the job was advertised nationally, a regional labor pool if the job ad appeared in regional publications, etc. To produce the measurements required by Revised Order #4, each federal contractor needed to produce availability analysis depicting the relevant labor pools for all job groups employed within the firm. For example, the firm might recruit nationally for accountants, so it would be required to use the national labor pool for accountants to estimate the percentage of minority and female accountants available in the nation, and in terms of recruiting cleaning help, it would determine what the local labor pool was for cleaning or maintenance personnel by minority status and sex. The chief sources of information used in the analysis were statistics produced by the U.S. Department of Labor, state labor agencies, and U.S. Census statistics. As federal contractors tend to be the larger firms in the nation, it was expected that they would have in their employment, or would hire, the people who could set up the measuring systems required by the order. Eventually, this did occur, but not without a great deal of grumbling. With more or less anguished expressions of pain, federal contractors gradually set up the monitoring systems which told them, and the regulatory agencies, how well their firms replicated the composition of the relevant labor pools within their own workforces.

The approach to affirmative action taken by the U.S. Department of Labor has been both an onerous and a highly conservative one—onerous in that each contractor has to establish its own statistical tracking system by determining what statistics it needed, locating those statistics, and weighing them in accord with its own policies. If jobs were filled primarily with people from outside the firm, relevant labor pool statistics depicting the outside labor force would count heavily. If the jobs were filled by promotion from within the firm, relevant internal workforce statistics would count heavily. The establishment and maintenance of such systems require sensitive interaction between the data analysis function, the policy setting function, and the recruitment and hiring function. Achieving this interaction has not been easy for federal contractors. As to the highly conservative aspect of the current system of affirmative action, relying on current employment statistics to set the standard for employment also sets the levels of expectation at the status quo. That is, contractors must only maintain the standard of hiring at the level of current availability. If affirmative action was supposed to eliminate historic patterns of discrimination, accepting the status quo in terms of the employment pattern hardly touches historic employment discrimination; it does nothing for all the people excluded from the higher paying jobs by the discriminatory policies and practices in the past. All past and present affirmative action programs focus on providing opportunities for those persons ready and qualified for employment. Therefore, an affirmative action benefit comes when, in the absence of better qualified applicants in the pool, a fully qualified minority group member or female applicant in the pool receives the job without being discriminated against. From that perspective, "benefit" carries a hollow definition. But taking the entire hiring process into consideration, that job applicant receives the affirmative action benefit by being told about the job in the first place and by being screened fairly in the second place. Prior to the passage of affirmative action type legislation, neither condition would have been promised.

Executive Order 11246 and its accompanying regulation, Revised Order #4, stand to this day as the major affirmative action impetus for the nation. As federal contractors tend to be large and numerous, these regulations affect a substantial portion of the national labor force: the millions of employees of the 250,000 federal contractors. Therefore, the labor force pattern has been changed significantly, even though these regulations do not apply to all employers. In fact, the great majority of employers are under no obligation to engage in any practice of affirmative action. Yet, non-discrimination is the law of the land in the United States. Any employment actions taken from an affirmative action perspective, from a race or color consciousness, or to remedy historic patterns which artificially separated male jobs and professions from female jobs and professions, must be taken on the basis of law. To be safe, affirmative action efforts should always be made in accord with procedures required by the Office of Federal Contract Compliance Programs in the U.S. Department of Labor. Entities which go off on their own, such as municipalities which establish their own affirmative action programs, tend to lose the legal suits charging them with discrimination. For example, the minority contractor set-aside program of the City of Richmond was rejected by the Supreme Court because it attempted to do too much without a sufficient basis, i.e., to take affirmative action without establishing an acceptable method for determining availability.[2]

Considering how restricted and closely regulated the field of affirmative action actually is, it is amazing how much controversy has been generated by the term. Since the inception of President Reagan's administration, these two words have generated an enormous discourse, much of it heated and much of it based, unfortunately, on ignorance of facts. The development of the system for computing goals and timetables for rectifying employment patterns not reflecting the relevant labor force seems to be the root cause for much of the fear and anxiety generated by the concept of affirmative action. Without much evidence, President Reagan interpreted the goal-setting requirements of Revised Order #4 as requiring hiring quotas despite the order's clarity on this fact. No federal contractor has ever been disbarred from doing business with the government because it has not accomplished a hiring goal. Every year, thousands of federal contractors fail to meet hiring goals and, as long as the failure is not caused by discriminatory hiring practices, continue to do business with the federal government. Zealous

OFCCP agents may pressure contractors to explain why they have not met the goals set by themselves as reasonable, but the agency as a whole has been extraordinarily passive in its enforcement activity in the area of goals. No federal contractor was ever prevented from doing business with the federal government on any basis until the administration of President Carter, and those instances occurred on the basis of extreme non-compliance and non-cooperation with all laws and regulations governing federal contracts, never for just the failure to meet hiring goals. The fear of affirmative action expressed by many people comes from some other quarter, not from the affirmative action regulations themselves.

THE CIVIL RIGHTS ACT OF 1964

The words "affirmative action" also appear in the major civil rights act passed by Congress in the twentieth century, namely the Civil Rights Act of 1964. Title VII of the Act exclusively addresses employment and provides protection against discrimination in hiring, firing, and all conditions of employment; yet, it uses the words affirmative action only once. According to section 706(g)

> If the court finds that the respondent has intentionally engaged in or is intentionally engaging in an unlawful employment practice charged in the complaint, the court may enjoin the respondent from engaging in such lawful employment practice, and order such affirmative action as may be appropriate, which may include reinstatement or hiring of employees, with or without back pay.[3]

A plain reading of this text indicates that one purpose for drafting the section was to reiterate the powers of the court, to state that the courts were expected to use their usual powers to deal with employers found guilty of discrimination. Title VII granted no new powers to the courts; all remedies enumerated in 706(g) were actions that courts regularly took when fashioning remedies to redress behavior that it had deemed illegal. In fact, the enumeration of remedies provided to the courts by

Title VII served to deprive the courts of a very important remedy: namely, the right to punish offenders. Normally, an accused individual or company found guilty of intentionally violating a federal statute expected punishment either in the form of imprisonment and/or fines. Title VII did not provide for such remedies. Instead of punishment, it focused on making the victim whole, restoring the victim to that place he or she would have achieved except for the act of discrimination. Therefore, affirmative action as conceived by Title VII represents actions ordered by the courts to restore the rights of victims of discrimination.

Thus, the two laws that attempt to deal with employment discrimination use the term affirmative action differently. In E.O. 11246, affirmative action constitutes positive steps that should be taken by an employer to confront the patterns brought about in the labor force by centuries of general societal discrimination. It accuses no one of discrimination, but simply asks everyone to take positive steps to eliminate it. In Title VII of the Civil Rights Act, affirmative action refers to the steps a legal remedy imposes upon a firm found guilty of discrimination. To a large extent, this initial differential use of terms causes confusion over what is meant by affirmative action. To federal contractors, the terms mean steps mandated to remain a federal contractor. This constitutes activity that might be burdensome, particularly when the system had to be developed from scratch, but which is essentially benign; a contractor must do nothing more than advertise a position, set up an appropriate system for measuring qualifications, and hire on the basis of the qualifications of the position (i.e., hire the best qualified, track progress on the basis of goals and timetables, and keep records to show how the employment decisions were made). Any non-discriminatory reason provided by the employer to justify an employment decision will ordinarily be accepted by a federal audit, if it seems reasonable and in tune with general employment practices. Revised Order #4 requires no activity that would be considered inappropriate by reasonable persons sympathetic to the ultimate goals of achieving equity in the labor force. On the other hand, employers found guilty of discrimination—many of whom do not feel guilty in violating the law—are forced to take strong measures to achieve compliance. These measures are imposed, not voluntary, and the courts are accustomed to having their decisions carried out to the letter. A number of courts have felt compelled to set employment quotas, such as ordering that a firm hire one Black person out of every four hires, to subdue recalcitrant employers like police departments, fire departments, and public utilities, particularly those in the South, which were prepared to use all means to resist or even fight a court order. All affirmative action quotas, in the true meaning of the word quota, were and still are imposed by courts on employers not only found guilty of discrimination, but also believed to be so recalcitrant by a judge that the only remedy available was to order a quota system which the court could monitor.

THE CONDEMNATION
OF AFFIRMATIVE ACTION

Using the term affirmative action to describe the few, sometimes harsh, remedies imposed on employers refusing to otherwise comply with the law has led or allowed persons to condemn affirmative action programs in general. The general condemnation of affirmative action is unfair because hundreds of thousands of affirmative action programs operate without quota systems, without depriving non-minority persons of their rights. These programs rely on extra attention, extra outreach, and extra care in designing systems so that they do not discriminate against members of groups historically excluded from opportunities. The objective of these programs is to eliminate the advantages of preferential treatment acquired by majority group members over the course of generations. It is impossible to sort out who has benefitted because a father or grandfather did not have to compete with a woman or minority group member for a slot in college or professional school or a relatively high-paying industrial job. It can be historically documented that certain groups have benefitted in just that manner. Anyone who would deny that groups in the United States have been treated unequally through the mechanisms of the law or social custom would have to deliberately ignore reams of evidence.

Because of a national history of discrimination, Congress passed a series of acts in the 1960s and 1970s with the goal of ridding the nation of the burden of inequality; to take some action to help those persons treated as outcasts or second-class citizens in the labor force because of their race, color, national origin, religion, sex, age, disability, or Vietnam Veterans' status—factors not related to their ability to do a job. These extra efforts impose a relatively small burden on majority group members and are only provided to people who are qualified to do the job. Not a single law, executive order, federal or state regulation of any kind provides any help to persons unqualified for employment. The protection provided to persons with disabilities specify to redundant degrees that they only apply to persons otherwise qualified for employment, and that the accommodation expected of the employer must be *reasonable* and cannot impose an undue hardship. All laws which deal with equal opportunity have been drafted with the objective of surviving the scrutiny of many legislators representing business interests and the interests of majority group members. All these laws represent compromise positions between the wishes of those clamoring for relief and the fears of those who might be adversely affected by relief given to others. Any attempt to portray the American legislative and judicial system as wild-eyed revolutionaries attempting to give away the store to Blacks, women, and various minority group members fails in its manifest absurdity. Anyone with any sense of history should recognize that the affirmative action programs being implemented in the United States are very moderate attempts to adjust a system which has gone considerably out of whack.

Despite the fact that government efforts at affirmative action are very modest, conservative, and tend to preserve the status quo, those group members who have acquired the education and skills necessary to enter the labor force are doing so in greater numbers. The growing numbers of middle class minority group members who leave minority neighborhoods where the poor continue to reside has produced concern that an underclass unreachable by affirmative action programs is developing and will eventually threaten the economic system of the nation. Certainly such a development portends ill for the nation but no blame should be attached to affirmative action. Rather, the blame appropriately rests on the lack of socially responsible programs to help educationally disadvantaged victims of poverty.

Affirmative Action Results

Affirmative action programs produce results. Obviously, if the game is zero-sum, any gain for one group means less for another group. But life does not appear to be a zero-sum game, at least in terms of the impact of the demographic changes occurring in the United States in the late twentieth century. Birth rate differentials and immigration patterns are rapidly changing the composition of the labor force. It has been predicted that by the year 2000 available white males could not begin to meet the demand that will exist for engineers in the U.S. The entrance of females and minorities into the engineering fields critically provides the necessary labor power to meet the minimum needs of the economy. Affirmative action programs that encourage women and minorities to enter the engineering fields may be the only things standing between a strong, viable economy and a major economic calamity. If the traditional pattern of exclusion is not broken in the fields of engineering, and not broken soon, the cost to the economy will be prohibitive. From this perspective, a strong commitment to affirmative action will be necessary to ensure the survival of the nation as a major producer of the world's goods. As the white male portion of the population shrinks, others, as occurred in World War II, will have to step in and take up their share of the productivity burden. Major corporations are aware of the dramatically changing demographics of the nation and have, since the mid-80s, supported affirmative action efforts in the labor force and in the educational arena. Many representatives of large corporations acknowledged that affirmative action practices had become a matter of survival at the same time that a strong negative reaction set in among persons with access to and influence in the media.

This produced the ironic situation of often large-scale media attacks on the underlying concepts of affirmative action just as corporate America began to expand its commitment to affirmative action programs with a focus on raising productivity by learning how to manage and motivate a diverse workforce. Companies guided by the bottom-line have, on their own, recognized the need to invest in programs that can produce solutions to the problems that emerge from managing a diverse workforce. There is a need to improve communication across cultural and linguistic barriers; a need to learn new motivational techniques which work for persons whose culture emphasizes values different from the majority culture; and a need to respond to the different sensitivities, etc. A diverse workforce, particularly one managed by white male managers, challenges America's way of doing business. But there is no other recourse. The die has been cast. The workforce for the early years of the next century has been born, and white males constitute a minority.

The principles of affirmative action hammered out in the federal agencies and the courts are moderate principles with the objective of gradual incremental change. In the 1960s, when these principles were first enunciated, they were promoted because they were fair and in accord with the founding principles of the nation. In the 1990s, it has been discovered that these principles are pragmatic and founded in the makeup of the actual and future labor force. When we started out on this course as a nation, we were doing the right thing. Now we find that affirmative action programs are necessary and absolutely essential to our economic survival. If we survive as a major economic force in the twenty-first century, it will be because we produce a labor force capable of surmounting the tearing pressures of difference by turning differences into strengths rather than weaknesses. In surviving as a productive power in the world, we will eventually outgrow the need for affirmative action programs because we will have achieved a unified labor force in which factors extraneous to ability will not interfere with productivity. It may take a long time to do it, but do it we must.

THE MYTHS OF AFFIRMATIVE ACTION

Let us now examine some myths that have grown up around affirmative action programs since the first days of designing and building the program.

MYTH 1: Affirmative Action Is a "Quota" System

The fear that affirmative action steps would result in the imposition of quotas to bring about the hiring of minorities emerged very early in the debate over making employment discrimination illegal. Opponents of the Civil Rights Act of 1964 pictured every conceivable abuse of the act, demonstrating some very vivid imaginations in their efforts to stop its passage. In the records of the congressional debate on the passage of Title VII, there are a number of references to the issue of possible imposition of quotas. On April 23, 1964, Senator Williams of New Jersey is quoted as saying:

> . . . it is also charged that employers, including farmers, will have to hire employees according to race to establish racial balance in every job classification; and it is said that quotas will be imposed, forcing businesses to hire incompetent and unqualified personnel. For some reason, the fact that there is nothing whatever in the bill which provides for racial balance or quotas in employment has not been understood by those opposed to civil rights legislation. Those opposed to H.R. 7152 [the house version of Title VII] should realize that to hire a Negro solely because he is a Negro is racial discrimination just as much as a "white only" employment policy. Some people charge that H.R. 7152 favors the Negro, at the expense of the white majority. But how can the language of equality favor one race or one religion over another? Equality can have only one meaning, and that meaning is self-evident to reasonable men. Those who say that equality means favoritism do violence to common sense.[3]

The cogent arguments of Senator Williams appeared to have little impact as Senator Allot of Colorado was forced to speak up on May 5, 1969.

> . . . I have heard over and over again in the last few weeks the charge that Title VII, the equal employment opportunity section, would impose a quota system on employers and labor unions. Here are two variations of the argument. One is that because Title IV specifically says that "desegregation" shall not mean assignment of students to public schools in order to overcome racial balance, and Title VII contains no such disclaimer in relation to employment practices, then it follows that Title VII is intended to require having to overcome racial imbalance in the workforce. The other variation is that an employer will hire members of minority groups, regardless of their qualifications, to avoid having any problems with the Equal Employment Opportunity Commission. The result either way, so the

argument goes, is that a quota system will be imposed, with employers hiring and unions accepting members, on the basis of the percentage of people represented by each specific minority group.

I do not agree with the argument. . . . I do not believe Title VII would result in imposition of a quota system. . . . But the argument has been made, and I know that employers are also concerned with the argument. I have, therefore, prepared an amendment which I believe makes it clear that no quota system will be imposed if Title VII becomes law.[4]

The amendment, adding clarifying language to Title VII, was passed. In spite of this, the claims and charges of quota systems continue to this day, though no employer has ever been found guilty of using a quota system to hire minorities or women.

A quota system was developed, however, by a university in attempting to admit minority students to medical school. In a case brought against this system, a man named Allan Bakke challenged the quotas used by the University of California at Davis.[5] The UC-Davis admission system was quite open about requiring sixteen places to be set aside for the admission of minority students despite the fact that white applicants with higher test scores and grade point averages might not be admitted in order to meet the quota for minority students. The University developed the system to combat the significant lack of Black or Hispanic physicians. The University was told by the Supreme Court that while it could take race into consideration in making admissions decisions, it could not establish a quota system to do so. The university could take affirmative action steps to locate and admit qualified minority students, but not at the expense of white applicants who the university acknowledged to be better qualified. Although this was not an employment case, the Supreme Court sent a loud and clear signal in 1978 that any kind of racial quota system not established by the courts would be unacceptable.

The fact that affirmative action programs were charged with being quota systems prior to the passage of civil rights legislation, and that they continue to be similarly charged despite the fact that no evidence supports that allegation in the 26 years since the passage of Title VII and the enactment of E.O. 11246, leads to the inevitable conclusion that the allegation needs no substance to survive. It survives, and even thrives, on an atmosphere of fear. The fear of big government combined with the fear that minorities will subject majority group members to their past transgression provide all too understandable bases for this fear. The media plays to this fear in the publication of many stories dealing with unsubstantiated charges of the existence of quota systems. In spite of the lofty claims in which newspapers and other forms of media wrap themselves, it is quite clear that playing to the irrational fears of people pays off handsomely in terms of readership and viewership. It is, therefore, unlikely that this issue will go away until the inevitable diversification of the labor force has progressed quite substantially and people no longer believe they have claims to jobs which might be challenged by counterclaims on the part of minority group members.

MYTH 2: Affirmative Action Causes the Hiring of the Unqualified

Related to the myth that affirmative action is simply a quota system under another name is the myth that thousands of unqualified people are forced on employers by laws and bureaucrats. Like the quota myth, no evidence supports this belief either. This issue was addressed very early by the U.S. Commission on Civil Rights. In a statement made in 1968 by C. H. Erskine Smith, Chairman of the Alabama State Advisory Committee to the CCR, it is pointed out that little has changed for Blacks since the passage of the Civil Rights Act because of, among other reasons, the need to meet employer-set qualifications requirements.

> In the area of employment, the Commission found in its three meetings in Alabama cities that indeed employers were aware of Title VII and its provisions. In some cases, employers had hired one or two Negroes in non-traditional jobs before or just after the effective date of the law. . . . The Commission found that a number of companies began using pre-employment tests and tests for upgrading near the time of the effective date of Title VII or whenever separate lines of progression or other discrimination provisions were eliminated. The Commission found that Negro high schools, de facto Negro vocational schools in Mobile and Huntsville and a Negro college were not turning out graduates who could meet the employer's qualifi-

cations, or were largely training students for traditional menial occupations formerly assigned to Negroes. On the other hand, the Commission found little evidence of really [sic] affirmative action on the part of employers to recruit, train, and employ Negroes. . . . Some of the space age industries of Huntsville were an exception. . . . However, it would appear that many of the Negroes employed in professional or upgraded positions with these industries were from outside Alabama. [The conclusion here is that these industries were hiring Black employees but only those who met the qualifications, meaning Black persons who received schooling outside of the South.][6]

Ample evidence exists that the passage of Title VII affected employment systems in an unanticipated manner. Employers are now forced to establish objective methods for developing criteria to determine what qualifications are necessary to adequately fill positions. These methods were not required before because no legal right to challenge hiring decisions, except in the area of collective bargaining, existed before Title VII. Since the passage of that act, however, a great deal of effort has gone into systematizing the setting of qualification standards culminating in the issuance of the testing guidelines called the "Uniform Guidelines on Employment Selection Procedures," adopted by the four major discrimination-monitoring agencies of the federal government in 1979. All firms of any size now use detailed descriptions of required and desired qualifications for all positions. While such a development is itself desirable in leading to better, more objective hiring systems, it tends to elevate qualification standards in the United States, not lower them as charged by critics of affirmative action.

One aspect of the development of devices for testing qualifications seems to support the claim that the laws governing equal rights cause the hiring of persons with fewer qualifications. As more and more tests began to be used after the passage of the Civil Rights Act of 1964, unanticipated patterns become obvious. Minorities, and sometimes women, were not scoring as well on some tests as white males. Although this fact caused some people to jump to the conclusion that this indicated that minorities and women were not as qualified as white males, test makers found themselves often unable to defend the validity or reliability of their tests when challenged in the courts, and test users could not defend the way the tests were being used. Any employee screening test must be shown to predict qualification better than chance, that is better than 50 percent accuracy. A test must show it can distinguish between potentially good employees and poor employees. People are surprised when they find out that tests are not as scientific or objective as believed. To many people brought up in educational systems predicated on the outcome of tests, challenging the validity of tests is almost unAmerican. Yet, as employers became more reliant on testing tools for screening applicants, more tests were challenged in the courts with the courts finding many tests being used inappropriately or inadequately designed to test what they purported to test. The lower scores achieved by minorities and women, therefore, did not mean they were less qualified to do the job. The scores may simply be products of the cultural differences that exist in our society. To get around the problem with tests, many employers simply set up separate pools of job applicants ranked according to test scores within each pool and selected the top candidates across the pools. This practice, known as "race norming," was outlawed by the Civil Rights Act of 1991. Employers are required to develop tests that fairly measure skills for jobs. This is proving to be a very difficult challenge.

The fundamental Supreme Court opinion on the use of tests is found in the landmark decision of *Griggs v. Duke Power Co.*[7] In a decision issued March 8, 1971, the Court established standards for judging the legal validity of tests used to make employment decisions. In this case, the Duke Power Company of North Carolina maintained a segregated system of employment, resulting in limiting Black employees to the lowest paid category of employment. In 1955, after the *Brown v. Board of Education* cases found that segregated educational systems violated the U.S. Constitution,[8] Duke Power abolished its segregated employment system, but at the same time, instituted the requirement of a high school diploma for all employees except those in the "labor" category, the category traditionally reserved for Black employees. In 1965, the company added the requirement that individuals also pass two aptitude tests to qualify for employment in the categories of jobs that were still completely held by whites. It also allowed workers in the labor category who lacked a high school diploma to transfer to inside, traditionally white-held jobs, if they passed both the Wonderlic Personnel test and the Bennett Mechanical Comprehension test. When challenged to defend the use of these tests, the company admitted that neither test had been designed to measure the ability to perform the jobs at Duke Power Company. The trial also found that the cut-off scores established by the company were those which approximated the national median for high school graduates. The effect of all this testing activity was to maintain a strictly segregated work force at the power company. According to the record, white employees were not adversely affected by these tests inasmuch as the percentage of white employees without high school diplomas who received promotions requiring high school diplomas approximated the percentage promoted with high school diplomas. According to the Court, " . . . neither the high school completion requirement nor the general intelligence test is shown to bear a demonstrable relationship to successful performance of the jobs for which it was used. Both were adopted without a meaningful study of their relationship to job-performance ability." The Court therefore concluded the following:

> Nothing in the Act precludes the use of testing or measuring procedures; obviously they are useful. What Congress has forbidden is giving these devices and relationships controlling force unless they are demonstrably a reasonable measure of job performance. Congress has not commanded that the less qualified be preferred over the better qualified simply because of minority origins. Far from disparaging job qualifications as such, Congress has made such qualifications the controlling factor, so that race, religion, nationality, and sex become irrelevant. What Congress has commanded is that any tests used must measure the person for the job and not the person in the abstract.[9]

In a 1975 testing case involving a situation similar to that at the Duke Power Company, evidence presented to the Court showed that a North Carolina paper mill used tests in spite of knowledge that some white incumbents of high ranking jobs could not pass the Wonderlic tests being used to screen employees for the lower ranking jobs.[10]

The Supreme Court has on a number of occasions approved the standards set by the Uniform Guidelines established by the regulatory agencies, and, therefore, feels it provided adequate standards to guide employers on the use of tests for non-discriminatory purposes. Employment qualification tests can be used by employers for legitimate purposes. Any employer who uses a test, however, must be ready to prove that the test used was appropriate for the job; that it measured reliably; and that it was applied correctly. Too many abuses have been found by the courts and, therefore, the courts carefully examine how tests are used by employers.

MYTH 3: Affirmative Action Was Designed as a Poverty or Social Welfare Program

Related to the myth that affirmative action programs force the hiring of the unqualified is the assumption that affirmative action is a poverty or social welfare program. This belief is probably based on the fact that Title VII was passed in the Johnson administration, during the so-called War on Poverty. Title VII was never part of the poverty programs introduced by the Johnson administration and was essentially developed under the previous Kennedy administration. Title VII was clearly designed to deal with discrimination, not with poverty *per se*. Neither was President Johnson's Executive Order designed as a poverty program. It was designed to eliminate historic discrimination. Obviously, if people are denied jobs or are relegated to the worst jobs in the economy, they will be poor. But if Congress had wanted to use affirmative action programs as anti-poverty programs, they would have required the establishment of training programs and avoided a system so totally reliant on full possession of all qualifications necessary for the job. All laws and regulations that have been adopted in the fields of equal employment opportunity and affirmative action provide rights of action only to individuals who meet all the qualifications for employment. To bring a case under Title VII, a person must show that he or she can make a prima facie claim. In a 1973 case challenging a hiring decision such a claim required the establishment of certain facts: (1) the person is a member of a group protected by law, (2) the person applied for a job and met the advertised qualifications for the job,[3] despite holding the relevant qualifications, the person was refused the job, and (4) the job remained open and the company continued to seek applicants for the job.[11] If claimants meet this standard, only then are they allowed to bring suits to *prove* by other evidence that they were discriminated against by employers.

Because affirmative action was never designed as a poverty program, it would be unfair to expect that it would have an effect on hard-core poverty. Yet, affirmative action programs are often attacked because hard-core poverty has not been eliminated. Affirmative action was designed to eliminate discrimination and discriminatory patterns that were stopping the entrance of minorities and women into the labor force. Although not enunciated explicitly in the act, the Civil Rights Act of 1964 was designed to stop the practices unfairly keeping people out of the economic mainstream, out of the middle class. All studies show that the purpose of the act is being accomplished. In terms of salaries, minority persons achieving at least a high school diploma are significantly better off than they were in the 1960s in comparison with the salaries earned by majority group members with high school diplomas. The picture is even brighter for persons with a college degree and most equitable for minorities with graduate degrees where almost all salary gaps produced by discrimination have been eliminated. When measured by the appropriate standards, affirmative action laws have produced significant changes in the patterns they were designed to change. The significant growth shown in the Black middle class is a direct testimonial to the efficacy of the Civil Rights Act and E.O. 11246. This growth could not have occurred under the old, unregulated system which deliberately and systematically excluded minorities from the higher paying jobs.

In recent years, fears have been expressed that affirmative action has brought about a split in the Black community along class lines. The tendency for people to self-segregate along economic status lines has always been evident in housing patterns. Affirmative action programs enabled qualified individuals to get good paying jobs which, in turn, enabled them to afford good housing. American society has always shown a tendency toward upward mobility, and that tendency is still manifest.

Few people remain in old, decrepit, dangerous neighborhoods when they can afford better. Affirmative action programs definitely contribute to the split between middle class Blacks and lower class Blacks in terms of geography. Such a split was inevitable if the laws were effective; its occurrence provides further evidence that the laws are effective. But rather than blame the effect on affirmative action, blame should lie with the lack of commitment to do anything meaningful to confront hardcore poverty. It is relatively easy to bring about the employment of persons who have education and skills. The real challenge is to educate and qualify the children of the poor so that they are equipped to rise as far as their talents can take them.

MYTH 4: Affirmative Action Constitutes Reverse Discrimination

As has been stated earlier, the law of the land is non-discrimination. All equal-opportunity, non-discrimination laws cut evenly, in all directions. A law disallowing discrimination on the basis of color protects persons with white complexions as much as it protects people of color. This should be obvious, yet based on the stated intentions of the law makers, the focus for the establishment of non-discrimination laws was to eliminate discrimination suffered by the people of color and by adherents of religions not considered mainstream. No legislator ever claimed that a law was needed to protect white persons or Protestants from racial or religious discrimination. Inherent, however, in the approach taken by Congress was protection for all. Congress did not draft a law that only applied to non-Caucasians or Catholics or Jews. Even though Congress started out with the concern for eliminating the type of discrimination actually found in this nation, they enacted laws that protected every member of every group regardless of race, color, religion, national origin, and sex. If a person could prove that he or she had been denied an employment opportunity because of being white, that person would be entitled to relief. Such claims have been made and won in cases like the aforementioned Bakke case.

The issue becomes more complicated when dealing with

affirmative action programs. Such programs introduce race-consciousness and sex-consciousness into the employment decision process. A company subject to E.O. 11246 is expected to take its goals seriously and attempt to fulfill them. On the other hand, employers are expected to stop short of reverse discrimination in meeting these goals. The courts have been unsympathetic to any employer who hires or promotes a less qualified minority candidate over a more qualified majority applicant, as in the cases cited above.

The landmark case which attempted to determine when race consciousness would be appropriate in affirmative action programs was decided in 1979 in *Steelworkers (USA) v. Weber.*[12] In this case, the Court had to decide the legality of an apprenticeship program developed within an Affirmative Action Plan, reserving 50 percent of the openings in a craft-training program for Black employees. The company, Kaiser Aluminum & Chemical Corp., admitted that its craft workforce was two percent Black in a workforce area that was 39 percent Black. Realizing how vulnerable its practices were to a suit, it had developed a well-designed AAP which included the apprenticeship program. The Court held:

> The purposes of the plan mirror those of the statute [Title VII]. Both were designed to break down old patterns of racial segregation and hierarchy. . . . At the same time the plan does not unnecessarily trammel the interests of the white employees. The plan does not require the discharge of white workers and their replacement with new Black hires. . . . Nor does the plan create an absolute bar to the advancement of white employees; half of those trained in the program would be white. Moreover, the plan is a temporary measure; it is not intended to maintain racial balance, but simply to eliminate a manifest racial imbalance.[13]

The standards enunciated in Weber have been used by the Supreme Court ever since to guide it in deciding whether affirmative action taken by employers is legal or not.

Another important case dealing with so-called reverse discrimination claims, but this time involving claims of discrimination on account of sex, was decided by the Supreme Court in 1987 in the case of *Johnson v. Transportation Agency, Santa*

Clara County, California.[14] In 1978, the Transportation Agency had adopted a voluntary affirmative action plan which, among other things, allowed the agency to take sex into consideration when deciding on promotions in traditionally segregated job classifications. When Mr. Johnson was passed over for a promotion in favor of Ms. Joyce, he sued on the basis of sex discrimination. At the time of the adoption of the AAP, none of the county's 238 Skilled Craft Worker employees was a woman. The agency admitted that women did not seek these jobs "because of the limited opportunities that have existed in the past for them to work in such classifications." The agency then drafted a carefully designed program which used appropriate labor pool information to set annual goals for these positions and explicitly disavowed the use of quotas. In 1979, the agency announced a vacancy for a roads dispatcher, and nine qualified applicants were interviewed for the position. The scores on interview ranged from 70 to 80 with Mr. Johnson achieving a 75 and Ms. Joyce achieving a 73. A second interview was conducted, and Ms. Joyce was recommended with both candidates ranked as "well qualified." The decision to hire Joyce took into consideration the fact that there were still no women in the Skilled Craft category four years after the adoption of the AAP. The Supreme Court decided that

> . . . the Agency appropriately took into account as one factor the sex of Diana Joyce. . . . The decision to do so was made pursuant to an affirmative action plan that represented a moderate, flexible, case-by-case approach to effecting a gradual improvement in the representation of minorities and women in the Agency's work force. Such a plan is fully consistent with Title VII, for it embodies the contribution that voluntary employer action can make in eliminating the vestiges of discrimination in the workplace.[15]

The courts have been assiduous in their role as protectors of the civil rights of everyone regardless of race, color, etc. It took a case as marginal as *Johnson v. Santa Clara* to establish that moderate use of sex consciousness in accord with a well-written plan would be accepted by the Supreme Court. Given the current makeup of the Court, it would be hard to predict how such a case would be decided in the future. In any event, high standards of proof are always required by the courts. If someone can meet those standards, it would be assumed that equity relief would be granted that person, whatever the form of discrimination. White victims of discrimination could expect equitable relief as could Black victims. The fact that very few reverse discrimination cases have been lodged, and that those that have are taken very seriously by the courts, should serve to reassure a reasonable person that there is little evidence of reverse discrimination in the land. The fact that this myth will not go away appears to be based more on fear than on reality. Like the myth of affirmative action quotas, there appears to be no need for evidence to support the myth. It feeds on itself and on pessimistic perceptions of human nature. Because certain groups suffered egregious discrimination over a long period of time, some people jump to the conclusion that laws protecting those groups from further discrimination would bring about discrimination against the former "masters." Such people do not understand how laws operate in this country. Laws are not used as a form of retribution. No law can be passed that seeks vengeance. Under our Constitution, laws must protect all citizens equally. Though only some citizens suffer discrimination on the basis of race, color, religion, national origin, sex, and disability, the laws designed to eliminate discrimination protect everyone. While this impartial approach may seem to lack perfect justice in the short run, in the long run such an approach will work to accomplish its end better than any approach which seeks to reward and punish. All individuals are better off in a nation with impartial laws. Short term programs like affirmative action better deal with the problems caused by societal injustice than the enactment of laws treating group members differentially. No matter how long it takes, when the effects of segregated, discriminatory systems have been eliminated, affirmative action programs will disappear leaving only equal opportunity laws to protect all.

MYTH 5: Any Qualified Minority Applicant Has To Be Hired

A corollary to the myth that affirmative action programs produce reverse discrimination is the belief that if a qualified minority person applies for a position, that person must be given the job. While it is impossible to know for sure what is in the mind of persons making hiring decisions, nothing in the law makes such a requirement. In E.O. 11246 and Revised Order #4, which spell out what is considered affirmative action, no requirement exists specifying that an employer hire any qualified minority over an equally qualified majority applicant. On the other hand, if any employer passes up a qualified minority applicant to hire another qualified applicant who is a member of a majority group, that employer might have to defend that decision before a federal or state agency or a court of law. In such an eventuality, the employer would have to enunciate a reason for making the choice, and that reason could not be based on race, color, etc. Such possible legal implications put employers on the spot. In many situations, employers have to make choices between two or more equally qualified job applicants. The law is clear, however, that the only rationales prohibited to an employer are race, color, etc. Therefore, if an employer enunciates any basis at all for making such a decision, the burden of proof remains on the claimant to show by a preponderance of the evidence that the rationale provided by the employer was pretextural. The courts do not take such a burden lightly. Evidence has to be presented that discrimination did, in fact, take place. Therefore, any employer who acted in good faith is unlikely to lose such a suit.

Although this is true, it gives small comfort to the employer who faces a suit with all of the ensuing costs in terms of time and money. Court litigation can be very time-consuming and expensive. An innocent party can be accused of discrimination. That is a fact of the way our legal system operates, not a fact of Title VII. To use this fact against anti-discrimination laws would be equivalent to saying that innocent people sometimes are accused of crimes and, therefore, criminal law is at fault. The best protection an employer can have against being falsely accused of discrimination is to maintain a non-discriminatory system of employment. This system will produce results that can be used by employers to defend themselves. Finally, employment discrimination cases are very hard to prove and are getting harder to prove as employers learn to understand how the law operates and the courts become more conservative. Any person who believes that he or she has been discriminated against has a very long and arduous road to climb to get to the end of the claim. If the system is hard on employers, it tends to be even harder on claimants.

This review of the myths and realities of affirmative action has attempted to provide information necessary to understand what is and is not affirmative action in the U.S. today. Although the field is a complicated one, affirmative action is taken very seriously by employers, federal agencies, and the courts. If the reader believes it is necessary to take steps to eliminate patterns of discrimination that have been produced by centuries of disparate treatment, nothing depicted herein will be considered alarming. If the reader believes that no race, color, or sex consciousness should enter into employment decisions, the information contained in this chapter should be useful in learning about how affirmative action operates, how carefully the courts have repeatedly examined the issue, and how carefully they continue to monitor the issue day-to-day. Affirmative action is implemented responsibly by using careful decision-making processes. Thousands of legal suits have dragged the courts into a continued review of the process. After a quarter century of development at a very slow and deliberate pace, it seems almost preposterous that the myths continue to stir up debate and sound and fury. The stakes are high; the future of this nation is literally at stake. Let us hope that the next quarter of a century brings about a resolution of the questions of discrimination in employment. Let us hope that employment discrimination on the basis of factors extraneous to ability to do the job disappears thoroughly and completely from the American workplace. If we do not hang on to that hope, the vista of the future is a frightening one.

REFERENCES

1. U.S. Equal Employment Commission, *Legislative History of Titles VII and XI of Civil Rights Act of 1964* (Washington, D.C.: GPO, 1968), p.4.
2. Crosson v. City of Richmond, [1978] 488 U.S. 438; 109 Sup.Ct. 706.
3. U.S. Equal Employment Opportunity Commission, *Legislative History of Titles VII and XI of Civil Rights Act of 1964*, p. 89.
4. Ibid. p. 88.

5. Bakke v. The Regents of the University of California, [1978] 438 U.S. 912.
6. U.S. Commission on Civil Rights, *Hearing Held in Montgomery, Alabama,* (April 27 - May 2, 1968), p. 20.
7. Griggs v. Duke Power Company, [1971] 401 U.S. 424; 91 Sup.Ct. 849.
8. Brown v. Board of Education, [1954] 347 U.S. 438; 74 Sup.Ct. 686.
9. Griggs, p. 426, p. 855.
10. Moody v. Albmarle Paper Company, [1975] 422 U.S. 405; 95 Sup.Ct. 2362.
11. Green v. McDonnell Douglas Corporation, [1973] 411 U.S. 792; 93 Sup.Ct. 1817.
12. Steelworkers (USA) v. Weber, [1979] 443 U.S. 193; 99 Sup.Ct. 2721.
13. Ibid.
14. Johnson v. Transportation Agency, Santa Clara County, California, [1987] 480 U.S. 616; 107 Sup.Ct. 1442.
15. Ibid.

5

Recruitment and Retention

Lucy R. Cohen

RECRUITMENT

To ensure that recruitment practices and policies meet the broader organizational goal of building a diverse multicultural workforce, several components of the traditional recruitment process need to be re-examined, and other non-traditional avenues need to be explored. In addition, it is imperative for hiring supervisors to be educated about non-discrimination and affirmative action policies, as well as be encouraged to examine their own work values and potential biases that may affect their individual judgments. Supervisors and managers at all levels must also value the building of a diverse workforce. Through education and administrative support, supervisors can begin to understand that different skills and experiences have a rightful place in libraries. We need to reflect the multicultural environment of our educational and research community and to provide the best possible service to that clientele.

To build a multicultural workforce, the following should be considered:

1. Review Position Description.

Position descriptions evolve over time and may reflect irrelevant, unimportant, or exclusionary historical baggage. Descriptions must encompass groups of candidates that could bring different experiences and skills that build the diverse workforce and meet the overall broader organizational goal. For example, prior library experience in a public service setting should be required for positions which could utilize broader public service experience. This small change would enrich and not limit the pool. A review of position descriptions and requirements should ask the following questions: 1) What is really needed? 2) What is the history of this position and its requirements? and 3) What alternative requirements—transferable skills and experiences—could open up and build the pool to reflect diverse backgrounds and experiences?

In reviewing the description, it is important to avoid describing the position with technical library jargon which may inhibit applicants from applying. For example, ads should not explicitly describe tasks performed on the circulation system or name the particular in-house system, but rather should simply describe the tasks so that anyone could understand what work would be performed.

The position description should not be loaded with so many desired qualifications that potential applicants would consider themselves unable to meet them all and *not* apply for the position. Candidates do not always view desired qualifications as extras, viewing them instead as measures of what supervisors really want. It is counterproductive to review the position for basic requirements, only to pad the desired qualifications.

2. Review Selection Criteria.

For every advertised position description, supervisors should articulate selection criteria and ways to measure them. Supervisors should have in writing how the pool will be assessed and how all decisions related to the search will be measured. This is basic personnel practice. However, supervisors must understand that selection criteria need not always measure most qualified. In many cases, someone with the most education and experience may not be the best qualified candidate for entry- or middle-level positions. It is important to create a good fit between the candidate and the position, to look at the best match and the potential to grow and develop in a position, and to avoid the pitfall of "most" experience and education.

3. Review Current Outreach Techniques and Incorporate New Ones in Order to Broaden the Pool of Applicants.

The pools of applicants must be continually assessed and evaluated as to the effectiveness of our current methods. Be creative in advertising locations; consider journals and newspapers with broad, diverse readerships, as well as ones targeted to specific minority groups. Consider directed mailings to minority groups such as ALA's Black Caucus. For support staff positions, consider directed mailings to campus and community minority groups. Other suggestions include considering personal contacts and referrals, taking every opportunity to personally invite candidates to apply; sending hiring supervisors or other personnel to Job Fairs and Placement Centers; and organizing special meetings such as brown bag lunches to explain promotional opportunities to current staff.

Overall, pools can be enriched by requesting self-identification and sharing resumes. One candidate may not be the best match for a particular position, but once identified, can be included in other pools.

4. Assessing the Pool and Interviewing Candidates.

Supervisors must be educated about interviewing techniques. The largest pitfalls stem from the interviewer's personal biases. Interviewers must recognize how our views and stereotypes, subconsciously or consciously, affect the interview and decision-making. For example, dismissing an Asian applicant prior to the interview on the unfounded assumption that their English language skills are not adequate to perform the work defeats recruitment efforts. All interviewers must value diversity as an organizational goal; we in libraries must reflect our multicultural community.

Possible considerations for assessing the pool and interviewing include the following:

1. Ensuring the interview pool of candidates is racially diverse; if not, question why and consider reopening the search, re-advertising, or re-examining the position description and requirements.
2. Being aware of potential interviewer bias and the unconscious basic need to hire a "mirror image."
3. Being aware of and open to differing cultures and communication styles.
4. Keeping communication lines open during the interview.

5. Review the Search File and Recommendation.

Once the interviews are completed and the recommendation is written with all of the appropriate justifications, an objective party, such as a representative from a Personnel Office or a higher level administrator, should review the file by asking questions such as:

- What was the pool like?
- Were qualified minorities interviewed?
- What efforts were made to include minorities in the interview pool?
- How was the decision made?
- Was "best" qualified or "most" qualified recommended?

We must challenge hiring supervisors to look at their pools and candidates with new lenses. We should coach and counsel hiring supervisors on alternatives.

6. Additional Considerations.

In addition to re-examining our traditional practices and policies, we should consider other avenues to accomplish our goals. The following lists different possibilities:

- Target of opportunity funding.
  Set aside bridging funds to assist individual units or departments which have identified outstanding minority candidates but currently lack vacancies.
- Provide training support.
  If an excellent candidate meets all minimum qualifications but lacks a desired extra, providing training support can encourage the supervisor to meet the overall administrative goal and build a more diverse workforce.
- Provide individual job counseling to minority candidates.
  Aggressively recruit minority candidates. Spend time explaining the recruitment process, which is often a maze, and provide assistance in matching skills and experience to individual positions.
- Intern programs.
  Consider internships that would provide candidates possessing no prior library experience with opportunities to gain that experience and learn more about libraries and librarianship.

The University of Michigan Library has established a successful intern program. The objectives of the program are to equip the intern with the initial basic training in library functions and office-clerical skills for a nine-month period, with two months training in clerical duties, three or four months in public services, and the remainder in a technical services setting. This training is supplemented with Human Resources and Development (HRD) course work and other special development based on individualized needs. The program also provides the training-intern additional on-the-job training, a broader view of branch and divisional libraries, and an opportunity to work closely with library supervisors by placing them in library units within the cluster and technical services for an additional nine to 15 months.

Our experience to date supports our initial assumptions that minority candidates lacking library specific-skills and experience can achieve their employment potential with the help of this type of structured training experience introducing them to the specialized world of libraries. Our experience also underscores the fact that this program not only benefits the interns but also provides staff development opportunities for their supervisors. We are, through this program, broadening and enhancing our supervisors' skills in managing a diverse, multicultural workforce.

- Recruit minority librarians and administrators who can serve as leaders and mentors.
- Recruit minority support staff.
  By mentoring our staff and providing them other incentives such as tuition support and release time to attend classes, we can recruit more minorities to the profession, thereby enriching all of our candidate pools.
- Recruit minority student assistants for temporary support staff positions.
  An aggressive program which encourages minority students to work in libraries provides multiple opportunities to meet our overall objectives. First, it adds an additional opportunity to diversify the workforce. Additionally, it enriches our pools for regular support staff should the student wish to seek a more permanent position. And it serves as an additional opportunity to recruit minorities to the profession.
- Travel to recruit.
  Consider traveling to recruit from different schools and colleges with diverse populations.

To meet overall goals, aggressive salary offers (and counteroffers), and review of other incentives such as housing, moving costs, and family care issues may also need to be considered.

RETENTION

The issues surrounding retention are a bit more difficult to describe. We at the University of Michigan have not had enough experience as yet to measure our success or to develop an intensive retention program. Our approaches have been limited to attempting to create a climate which supports diversity, developing and maintaining a strong educational program for staff, and paying attention to other issues such as growth and development of staff. The following highlights potential action, though it is important to note that constant evaluation and examination must occur before an organization can assess change and program success.

1. Create the Climate that Supports Diversity

All staff within the organization need to understand the library's goals in this area. At the University of Michigan Library, administrators clearly articulate their vision: as a crucial member of the higher education community, we must create an environment which values diversity as another aspect of true intellectual and academic freedom. Our educational programs support that vision and further act upon the need for our staff to grow in their understanding of differences, specifically as it pertains to their working together as part of a multicultural diverse workforce and to the services they provide to a diverse community.

Additionally, managers need to recognize their special roles. They must develop skills which allow them to effectively manage people different from themselves, as well as provide leadership within their individual departments. Managers have the extra responsibility for setting the tone and providing the support for valuing diversity.

In creating a climate that values diversity, it is important to continually assess the current climate and barriers that prevent the organization from moving ahead. All policies need to be examined, since old rules may no longer apply. Institutional values and norms need to be questioned.

As part of this assessment, the University of Michigan Library sponsored a staff development program, "An Ebony View of the Ivory Tower: A Program for People of Color." The program's intent was for library staff of color to explore some of the mainstream cultural and work norms and to identify barriers to success. The program was well attended and uncovered special concerns held by staff of color, such as:

- No chance of higher advancement or limited opportunities for promotions.
- Lack of management training programs.
- Stereotypes still exist and are highly visible.

- People of color seem to have to change their personalities in order to adapt to their work environment.
- Lack of understanding in religious differences and holidays that only support a Christian culture.
- Everything is led by white people—even the diversity programming.
- White people do not have a cultural understanding of Black people.
- Supervisors are given too much discretion.
- Rules are purposely made so that interpretation can be ambiguous.
- Blacks are afraid to hire Blacks for fear of being criticized.
- Dissemination of information—getting information second-hand, etc.
- Exclusion from the old boys and girls networks, socially and professionally; only Blacks who conform or assimilate are allowed.
- Lack of knowledge and *respect* for cultural differences—do not want to understand.
- No mentoring, formally or informally, and there is a lack of adequate mentor pools.

The output from this workshop was shared with top-level administrators and middle-level managers. It is important for organizations to provide opportunities to assess the problems and find vehicles for addressing them. Advisory committees need to pay special attention to these issues.

Additional considerations for creating a climate that supports diversity are

- Incorporating diversity into goals and planning.
  All staff should be encouraged to articulate goals and action plans which will assist them in meeting overall objectives. The formal mechanism of goal setting provides opportunities for staff members to evaluate their job functions and determine, for each one, how diversity can be incorporated and successfully measured.
- Institutionalize programs and committees.
  It is important for diversity programs to become part of our

everyday work and not be viewed as temporary in nature. Funding for these programs should be part of the general funds base budget. Examples of programs and committees that have been institutionalized at Michigan and further described in this and other chapters are:

- Training-intern program.
- Amity program.
- Diversity Committee.
- Diversity Librarian.
- Peer Information Counseling Program.

2. Educate Staff

A wide range of programs educating staff on valuing diversity should be developed. Such education promotes better understanding of differences and a greater sensitivity to the possibility that many of our assumptions about people are likely based on stereotypes. We, as staff members, also need a better understanding of our own personal values and biases and how they may affect our behaviors.

A key part of any staff development program is the training of supervisors and managers. Supervisors and managers have the additional responsibility to build skills which allow them to manage in a diverse workplace. They need to identify workstyles and explore how they might be related to culture; examine their own biases, perceptions, and expectations about work and explore how these will affect their managing of others. Most importantly, supervisors and managers need to develop better mentoring skills:

- Share information and informal rules.
- Provide growth opportunities.
- Provide clear performance expectations and coach appropriately.
- Foster open communication and be willing to discuss issues and value differences.
- Understand different cultures and be willing to adapt policies and procedures.

3. Other Considerations

• Promote growth and development of staff of color.
Consider special mentoring programs which allow colleagues
outside of the staff members' department to provide insights
into the organization and broader perspectives. Networking
or coalition groups also support the broader perspective and
provide opportunities for concerns to be aired and possible
solutions to be explored. An example of such at the University of Michigan Library is GALLA (the Gay and Lesbian Library
Association).

It is imperative to also examine opportunities for upward
movement within the organization. A true multicultural organization not only emphasizes diverse representation, but
also ensures equitable distribution of power and influence.

• Assess why staff of color leave the organization.
Consider an exit interview program which would attempt to
evaluate why staff leave.

• Recognize special needs and attempt to meet them.
To ensure retention, try to identify special needs and aggressively pursue meeting them. Some possible special needs may
include:

   1. salary counter-offers,
   2. altered position responsibilities, and
   3. flexible schedules.

6

Creating a Multicultural Environment in the Library

Frances E. Kendall

I have studied racism most of my life. As a white Southern woman, I learned early that skin color is a major determinant of one's access to privileges and resources. I sat anywhere on a bus, ate at any restaurant, went to any theater, and moved freely and with relative safety in any part of town; none of those things was true for my contemporaries whose skin was a different color than mine. My formal work on racism began in 1966 with my involvement in the National Student YWCA. There, I joined with women of color and other white women in a struggle to bring about personal and institutional change. As a consultant today, I find my methods affected by two lessons I learned at that time: as individuals, we can change our attitudes—even those we have held for most of our lives; and fundamental organizational change can be made when we work with colleagues committed to long-term change.

ELEMENTS OF A SUCCESSFUL TRANSITION TO A HOSPITABLE MULTICULTURAL WORK ENVIRONMENT

As an organization moves toward providing a successful multicultural environment for its employees, nine elements must be put in place. The more articulate a library is on these issues, the more likely it will become a hospitable, efficient, effective workplace.

1. The organization must believe it, and the people in it can change.

This is basically a mind-set. In the best of circumstances, a library decides to deal with the issues of diversity to better serve its patrons and therefore recognizes that it needs to recruit and retain a diverse work force as well as assess its collection and its outreach. Even if the impetus for this effort is less than optimal—if, for example, the community pressures the library to change—the effort merits positive promotion. Messages from top administrators, workshop, and forum publicity, and staff involvement build awareness, enthusiasm and commitment as the long-term plan is created. However, such campaigns should not underplay the complexity of the subject nor the discomfort inherent in diversity discussions and actions.

2. The organization must address diversity at the personal and institutional levels concurrently.

Valuing diversity is an integral organizational issue, not simply a staff development problem. An organization making the transition from homogeneity to heterogeneity must evaluate not only its policies, procedures, culture but also the personal attitudes of its individual employees. Often, heads of organizations believe successful management of diversity simply means ensuring that staff members are sensitive to one another and get along well. While a harmonious workplace is important, that harmony often comes at the price of stifling real communication about differences. For lasting change to occur, the administration must revise policies and procedures to encourage diversity of thought and approaches to doing things. At the same time, the staff needs training in talking with one another about differences. For example, a manager once sought sensitivity training for a staff member who constantly told jokes about women. When asked how long this behavior had been going on, the manager responded, "Oh, for years." The organization as a whole needed help; as long as its culture continued to tolerate the man's behavior, he had little incentive to change and less to sustain any improvement. Efforts must concurrently change the behaviors tacitly permitted and the policies pertaining to acceptable behavior.

3. **Top management must genuinely and seriously commit to an on-going examination of its own attitudes as well as its policies and procedures.**

The organizations most successful in working toward truly hospitable climates for all employees are those with senior-level managers genuinely committed to a diverse organization. These managers know they serve as models for the rest of the staff and continually probe their own attitudes about race, gender, sexual orientation, class, age, physical ability, religion, and culture. They are consistent in changing the policies and procedures that obstruct achieving a diverse workplace. By providing such a model, a senior manager sends the staff a clear message that the organization is serious about this effort.

4. **The organization must view diversity as a long-term, multifaceted, continual process, not as an event or a quick fix.**

Generally speaking, after an organization identifies a need, it figures out a way to meet that need. If a library realizes it needs to be computerized, the staff works together to make that happen. Though a long and arduous task, computerization has a beginning, a middle, and an end. If the ceiling leaks, it gets fixed. But creating an effective multicultural workplace is an abstract process, not a concrete event; no patch will fix this situation. The library can hire a more diverse staff, but the retention process has no end. Managers and staff can acquire new skills, but there is always more to learn. Individuals can adjust their attitudes and behaviors, but lifelong prejudices take lifetimes to erode. The University of Michigan Library has worked for the past few years to create a multicultural environment through examining and changing recruitment and hiring policies, allocating money for diversity efforts, and planning and implementing many programs. The Library received a University award for its work in diversity, and still it continues to struggle to become a better workplace for all while responding to the needs of its increasingly diverse patron population. Their ongoing process has made small and major accomplishments along the way. The successful organization includes diversity in the fabric of its mission, making it integral to every aspect of the workplace.

5. The organization must expect and be willing to deal with discomfort and resistance.

Working on issues of racism, sexism, homophobia, and other forms of institutionalized discrimination is extremely threatening and inevitably raises anxiety in the organization. Yet, a committed, on-going effort can push past the problems to become a more effective, efficient, and better place to work in the long run.

People function concurrently at three levels: the personal, the interpersonal, and the organizational. To bring about organizational changes, we must examine behaviors at each level. Addressing diversity at the personal and interpersonal levels requires that we inspect our stereotypes and prejudices and the ways our attitudes affect our behaviors and interactions with others. Because racism and other forms of institutionalized discrimination taint every aspect of an organization, each part of the organization must locate and remove barriers to a successful multicultural organization.

Self-examination frightens most of us; change unsettles us. Inevitably, some staff members resist these efforts. The administration can effectively confront resistance with a two-pronged approach: a clear and consistent message that efforts will continue despite the uncomfortable process, accompanied by a strong reassurance that the staff are valued, integral parts of the work. By expecting resistance and tackling it as it arises, managers at all levels stay on course, seeing the ups and downs not as aberrations, but as a natural part of the process.

6. The organization must not avoid discussions on institutional racism when addressing diversity and multicultural environments.

Valuing diversity is filled with complexities. Our society, by its structure, gives privileges to some that it does not give to others. Built into our institutions are policies and methods that affect us differently depending on our skin color, gender, sexual orientation, religion, and class. For example, several recent studies show that a person of color, particularly an African American, is far less likely to get a housing loan than a white person. All circumstances being the same, a white person is at least twice as likely to get the loan. That does not mean that all whites purposely hoard access to power and resources so that others cannot have them. Unfortunately, it is usually far more complicated and less intentional than that. Racism so pervades our society that those not faced with it daily often do not see it. As a result, plans for a diversity program often focus only on cultural differences, ignoring the prejudice and institutionalized discrimination—the key impediments to working well across racial lines. While we must learn how our cultural heritage creates difference in the ways we do things, it is not enough. Nor is it honest to pretend that if we all got along well together there would be no more problems. For an organization to genuinely address differences, it must confront the inequities brought about by its own institutional racism as well as the discomfort engendered by differences in cultures and backgrounds.

7. The organization must develop a long-term plan for achieving diversity.

No successful creation of a multicultural environment occurs without a long-term plan. Before beginning to change, the organization must assess its climate: how staff members feel about the library's diversity efforts; what new tools staff members need to work well with colleagues and patrons different from them; and what new skills managers need to lead a diverse work force (or a homogeneous work force in the process of becoming more diverse).

A long-range plan can then be designed to address the identified needs and move the organization to the next stage. With such a plan, the organization can determine how and when to work on different aspects of diversity, rather than taking on all issues at once. Tackling too many issues concurrently waters down the importance of each issue. That does not mean that some issues lack bearing on the health of the organization. Instead, each major area of concern should be addressed fully rather than lumping them together to treat racism, sexism, heterosexism, and class and religious discrimination the same.

8. The organization must develop a core staff willing to commit time and energy to bringing about a hospitable work environment for all people.

Rather than being in place when the effort begins, the core staff develops over time. Frequently, this process begins with a small number of people committed to improving the climate of the library, and as they work together, they involve more people in the various aspects of programming, skill-building, and the evaluation and changing of policies and procedures. The core group must include staff from different levels and areas of the organization so that the work and the enthusiasm get spread throughout the organization.

Every staff member cannot be expected to whole-heartedly support this effort; interest and commitment will vary among them. Some resistance to the changes will inevitably occur as the library climate adapts to its new goals and concerns about diversity.

A critical mass of committed people has no set number of people or even a specific percentage. In a small library, it might be five or six people; in a large university library with a staff of 285 people like the University of Michigan, it could be 35 to 50. The goal is to have enough people heavily involved so that the work does not rest with a few people with full-time staff responsibilities in addition to their involvement in this undertaking.

9. The organization must know that its diversity activities will mirror its other activities.

An often forgotten organizational phenomenon predicts an organization will respond to a new effort as it reacts to every other effort. Similarly, the feelings and sentiments present in the organizational climate will find expression in the work striving for diversity. For example, if the majority of the staff looks forward to new ways of doing things in general, they will likely be enthusiastic about becoming more diverse. On the other hand, a pervasive low morale will greatly affect transitional efforts. Any on-going conflict between staff and administration will temper response to a plan devised on one side or the other. Making changes to create a hospitable workplace for people different from those currently employed will certainly make a happier atmosphere for all who work there. However, a library cannot heal all its organizational wounds simply by working on diversity.

THE USE OF CONSULTANTS

Consultants serve several purposes in helping an organization make the transition to a multicultural workplace. The obvious reason to hire a consultant is to gain expertise. In automating a library, specialists evaluate how comprehensive and tailored the plans are. Work on racism requires similar planning and evaluation, especially since it carries greater risk than other change efforts. In the diversity process, the organization asks staff members to confront long-held attitudes, to talk about subjects previously deemed as impolite to discuss, and to begin changing how they interact with others, how they manage, and how they recruit, hire, and retain their staff. If someone we know, perhaps even our manager, asks our views on these things, we fear an honest answer risks adversely affecting our relationship with them. An outside consultant, however, can say and hear the unmentionable. Further, a person unconnected to an organization—without any investment in protecting the organization or the people in it—often gets a clearer view of what is going on and the best way to address those issues.

A consultant relies heavily on the internal people with whom she or he is working. Internal leaders play a crucial role in the transition to a truly diverse organization and operate as the consultant's lifeline. A consultant's role is intermittent; staff members remain there to plan and carry out programs, talk with and listen to staff, serve as a liaison between staff and administration, and keep issues of diversity on the front burner.

STEPS TO CREATING A HOSPITABLE MULTICULTURAL CLIMATE

1. Assess the library climate using both formal and informal measures:

- Conduct interviews.
- Examine reports and other written information about the organization.
- Identify other issues within the organization that might affect the diversity effort.
- Look at the library in the context of the whole university.

Any change effort begins with assessing where the organization stands. Such an assessment gathers information about current employee attitudes and perceptions and begins to introduce the notion of change to the whole staff. For an external consultant, this step not only provides much-needed information about the organization but also initiates a relationship with the staff.

The assessment step should include at least four elements, beginning with interviewing people who work in the organization. This can be done in a variety of ways: hold focus groups to identify issues in the organization, meet with administrators individually to get their perspectives, and talk to staff at all levels to hear their concerns.

Information from a different perspective can be gathered by examining reports and other written information about the organization. Such materials reveal how the library communicates about itself to others. What do written materials say, for example, about the issue of diversity? Does recruitment publicity stress the commitment to a diverse staff? Do the messages imply a welcoming and hospitable library environment to new employees and patrons? How are formal rules presented to newcomers? How do they find out about the informal rules?

The assessment must also identify other factors in the library that might affect the work on diversity. Two examples clarify this point. When one organization wished to initiate an all-staff training on diversity, this step reminded them that the staff had responded negatively to previous work on affirmative action. Before beginning anything new, they had to do some clean-up work. Another organization—in the midst of building a new library, automating, and hiring a new director—found these major endeavors would complicate the start of a new program.

There is never a perfect time to embark on a new program, but trying to do everything at once is as foolish as waiting until nothing else is happening. Only a look at the total picture will determine what will impinge on the work on diversity.

Finally, any library operating as a part of a larger organization, such as a university or a government office, must assess itself in that context as well. In 1988, the president of the University of Michigan issued what he called the Michigan Mandate—the order for the University to become a multicultural community. This mandate came in the wake of much campus unrest and several serious racial incidents. Acting in that context, the Library initiated its work with at least verbal support from the University. In many instances, however, a library will not work in such a supportive environment. More likely, a library may lead the institution's transition to a multicultural community. In a less positive scenario, it might walk alone in an environment that is hostile to such a move. None of these contexts make the process impossible; it is simply important to know what lies ahead before beginning.

2. Create a long-range plan and establish goals.

After an organization assesses its initial state, it should determine what it wants to achieve in three to five years. For example, a library with a fairly homogeneous staff and little past focus on the issues of diversity might decide that within three to five years it wants to have people of color working at all levels of the organization and wants diversity issues built into the staff evaluation process. With these goals clearly defined, concrete steps can be then planned, implemented, and measured.

Another library with an already diverse staff may want to rectify lingering perceived or real inequities: staff of color feeling they have been passed over for promotions; gay and lesbian staff believing their concerns are not being taken seriously; older staff thinking they receive less training and development

than their younger colleagues; or Jewish staff angry because the library continues to celebrate only Christian holidays. These cases call for a different long-term goal: to create a truly hospitable environment for all of the people who work in the library. The resulting plan might include training sessions about specific diversity aspects with an emphasis on retaining these people by responding to their specific needs. A library should also look at the dynamics of the organization that ostensibly have nothing to do with race, gender, age, sexual orientation, or religion, being seen solely as management issues. Such dynamics include the typical split between librarians and non-librarians, communication patterns among staff and between administrators and staff, and the ways decisions are made. The consolidated nature of organizational life permits no assumptions that patterns affecting one aspect will not affect all aspects.

Still another library might serve a community that is rapidly changing demographically, creating a sudden change in patrons and their needs. One long-term goal might be to radically change the collection to include more books written in languages other than English. Related steps may include hiring new staff from emerging cultures, requiring some current staff to take language courses, translating library signs into several languages, and developing on-going staff training in dealing with people of different cultures as well as classes exploring the specific cultures represented in the new population group.

No one set of needs, no one formula, exists for creating a multicultural organizational environment. Each long-term plan stems from the unique needs of a specific library.

3. Select a group of employees to work on diversity and prepare them to work together as models and facilitators.

A library diversity committee comprises a group of 12 to 15 individuals selected and recruited for their willingness to work on diversity issues and for their own diversity in job classification, race, gender, age, sexual orientation, religion, and so on. The group should contain people from the administrative assistant level to the assistant or deputy director level for three reasons: to encompass a range of ideas and opinions from

throughout the library; to provide the opportunity for supportive senior managers to hear the perspectives of people they
might not talk to regularly; and by including people with a direct
line to the director, to apprise the director of what is going on
both in the committee and in the library. The suggested diversity of the committee is intended not to create *representatives*
from each group (that is, people speaking for their groups) but
to bring together a collection of people who, partially because
of their differences, have much to share with and learn from
one another.

Diversity committee members have three roles: to advise
the administration, to educate and model for other staff members, and to participate in and sometimes organize diversity programs. As advisors to the administration, committee members
keep the director aware of the organization's climate, raise issues they have heard discussed in the library, and report incidents that otherwise might go unmentioned.

As models, committee members demonstrate that open discussion of sensitive issues enhances teamwork. Diversity aside,
all organizations strive for effective operation. The University
of Michigan's Library Diversity Committee began with team
building and facilitator training. A three-day retreat gave members the opportunity to get to know one another, to begin talking about issues related to diversity, and to gain new skills in
group facilitation. Shortly after that, they served as small group
facilitators in workshops for the entire staff.

The diversity committee also participates in the library's
diversity programs; despite their committee positions, they still
retain their non-committee status as colleagues and peers and,
as such, play a double role in changing the organization.

The library diversity committee does not necessarily contain all of the library's primary movers and shakers. They do
not organize and run all of the programs unless their job descriptions clearly assign them to do so. People burn-out when the
organization expects the most committed to bear the majority
of the responsibility and work to make changes happen. To fight
burn-out, committee members need periodic training on issues
they want to address. Such training rejuvenates them and
deepens their relationships with one another. Group members
also need on-going discussions about the dynamics within the

group and the implications of working in such a diverse group. For example, a library plans to celebrate Martin Luther King Day. In selecting the speaker for the library, the African Americans on the committee want to choose an African American, the Latinos suggest a Latino, and the gay man and lesbian on the committee want a gay person of color. The issues of whose oppression is greater, whom Dr. King stood for, and how to best present the topic of diversity to the library and the university sit squarely before the committee members. They could, of course, choose to ignore the thorny questions and simply talk about what speaker to bring to campus. But, in doing so, they would miss the opportunity to talk about issues that would enhance their communication in the long run. The committee models for the rest of the library in finding fruitful ways to discuss differences; the skills learned in committee meetings spread throughout the library as committee members converse with their units.

Too frequently, staff members are expected to become diversity trainers overnight. The incredible complexities involved in exploring the effects of attitudes on behaviors receive little recognition, increasing the potential that a situation will become unmanageable. People, particularly people of color in a predominantly white organization or women in a male-dominated organization, take a risk when they push colleagues to consider alternate views. Using an outside consultant as a facilitator, at least in the initial stages of the long-range plan, minimizes negative repercussions.

4. Begin training sessions with staff.

All staff members, regardless of rank and job description, need tools to address issues pertaining to differences. No one automatically, if ever, knows everything about these matters. Managers and supervisors need additional skills to better manage a diverse workplace (or a workplace in the process of becoming more diverse). Therefore, at varying points, the entire staff should be involved in workshops on diversity.

There is no one right order to set up these staff workshops, but good examples can be found in other organizations. For instance, the University of Michigan's Library Diversity Committee followed its initial retreat with an all-staff convocation and then eight three-hour workshops during one week. By the week's end, virtually every staff member had been involved in a workshop. Most managers and supervisors later attended an eight-hour session on managing a diverse work force. Over several years, the Library has held other workshops and programs focusing on various aspects of diversity. Additionally, sessions for new staff members introduce them to the Library's commitment to diversity.

Another organization chose a different route. Their process began with a two-day senior management retreat on diversity, part examining personal attitudes and behaviors and part creating a three-to-five-year plan for the organization. They then hosted a two-day retreat for their Diversity in the Workplace Committee, focusing on building a strong group, exploring racism, sexism, homophobia, and heterosexism, and drawing up the committee's initial plan of action. Both the senior managers and the Diversity Committee continued to meet in day-long planning sessions.

A fairly small public library chose to start with an all-day session for full-time employees, a half-day session for part-time employees, and a planning session for managers. A later one-day session for management, like all sessions, was tailored to meet their specific managerial and community needs. Also, further work was done with full- and part-time employees.

All-day workshops can be much more effective than those lasting only three or four hours. In an interactive day-long workshop, participants have the time to do real problem solving and leave feeling practiced in some new skills. A half-day session does not allow time to test new information. Before one can leap to problem-solving, one first has to explore one's attitudes. That takes time.

A final possible training method begins with an all-staff session (if the staff is small) and then continues with a series of two-hour sessions for all staff members on specific topics. In one library, the shorter sessions were on homophobia, sexism, programming for people using English as a second language, and "Us and Them"—the friction between administrators and staff, between librarians and non-librarians, and between staff and patrons.

There are some guidelines to keep in mind when initiating these sessions. First, there is no standard way to carry out a training program. Any effort a library makes should be designed specifically to meet the needs of that library, rather than following a program designed for another organization. Second, senior-level managers must be involved from the beginning so that they commit to the process and have input concerning the design. Third, some training should involve the entire staff in order to bring everyone up to par on diversity issues and skills. Fourth, sessions should be designed to provide managers with specific additional tools needed to recruit and retain a diverse workforce. Fifth, all work must be on-going at every level so that the organization's commitment remains clear.

5. Build diversity into the organizational structure.

Institutionalizing diversity means infusing it into every aspect of the organization, into policies and procedures, and into the formal and informal culture of the organization. This essential step ensures the effort will not stop when key movers and shakers leave the library or get burned out, when resistance increases, or when things go so well that the organization begins to feel it has finished the job and starts to rest on its laurels. Concretely, this step involves looking at the formal culture of the library: hiring, firing, coaching, and evaluating all staff. It includes examining the library's informal culture: the ways staff socialize and celebrate, the patterns of communication, how comments and jokes are answered, and how the informal rules are communicated and to whom. It means being conscious of the ways that new people integrate into the organization, how they are welcomed, made to feel at home, trained and supported in the first year. For example, a person of color taking a new position at a library in a predominantly white community needs help finding housing in a welcoming neighborhood. Paying that kind of attention to a person's first months gets any new employee off to a good start. The smart organization works to mitigate complexities as a part of procedure, rather than allowing the transition to a new situation to occur haphazardly.

A library can build the work on diversity into its structure in many ways. Integrating the issue of diversity into the evaluation process for all staff sends a clear message that managing diversity is not an option but a necessity in order to succeed. Creating an on-going budget line for diversity efforts weaves it into the fabric of the institution rather than making it a fringe effort. Setting up a diversity committee, doing a little bit of training and programming, and then taking the program out of the budget guarantees failure. Efforts to recruit and hire a more diverse staff can be strengthened by carefully analyzing how and where one advertises and how job descriptions are written and by delineating how a new person will fit into the organization. If it is expected that some staff of color carry the bulk of the work on diversity, their job descriptions should say so. Otherwise, they potentially become saddled with two jobs: the job they were hired to do and the one expected of them because of who they are. The library's written materials should describe its commitment to diversity, and that information should be updated regularly. The library's newsletters should carry a column devoted to some aspect of diversity every month to keep its concerns in the minds of both patrons and staff.

Confining responsibility for diversity work to the staff development and programming arenas of the library poses a great hazard to a successful transition to a multicultural environment. In limiting the scope of the workforce diversity effort to staff development, the organization supports the notion that all of the needed changes rest in the laps of individuals as matters solely of personal prejudice. In assuming instead that organizational culture changes purely by designing great programs, one underestimates the insidious qualities of racism, sexism, and other forms of institutionalized discrimination. Quality programs and development of new skills in staff are indeed crucial to the success of any effort toward diversity, but there is more. Even if the personnel office carries out the initial work on managing and valuing diversity, it should be considered as part of the library's long-range plan with the responsibility designated to a senior administrator.

Creating an hospitable multicultural environment is a long and complicated process. By using these steps as guidelines, a library prepares for the changes that need to take place, rather than letting them occur haphazardly. Talking openly about these steps with the staff underscores the commitment to valuing diversity in all parts of the organization.

THE EVALUATION PROCESS

One of the most difficult aspects of creating a multicultural environment in a library is evaluating progress. The following questions must be addressed.

What Factors Complicate Evaluation Efforts?

The Difficulty of Measuring Attitude Change

One of the most frequently cited goals for a diversity program is changing the attitudes of the staff. Though an appropriate desired outcome, it is not an easy one to assess. Measuring people's attitudes on race, gender, or sexual orientation has always been an extremely complicated and questionable proposition. It becomes even more difficult as people become more sophisticated about what is permissible to say and what is not. We know, for example, not to say that women are not strong enough to be library directors or that people of color are not smart enough to hold key positions in an organization. Rather, we cloak our attitudes in less obvious phrases such as, "the Board would have a hard time respecting a woman's perspective" or "he [a Black man] would not fit in with our staff." If anything, people often more willingly express their negative attitudes about gender than about race and feel little compunction in talking about their discomfort with or dislike of gay men and lesbians.

The Lack of a Discrete Beginning and Ending of the Task

Because changing a library's culture is an on-going process, not a one-time event, there is no discrete beginning or end to learning new ways of doing things as there might be putting in a new phone system. Just broaching the subject with the staff and managers moves the organization to a different place than it was before that mention, making it difficult to get truly clean information about where the library stands before beginning to act on diversity.

The Isolation of the Library Experience From the Outside World

Anything a library does about diversity is affected by the events and prevalent attitudes in the larger context in which the library exists—the university, the community, the country, and the world. Evaluation of the diversity program must take this larger context into account. For example, as senior managers initiate sessions to look at how racism is reflected in the library, racial violence erupts on campus. As a result, the staff becomes extremely reluctant to discuss the issues and resists participating openly in the program. A limited interest in the sessions could be interpreted as a lack of concern about racial issues. That certainly is one possibility. However, keeping the larger context in perspective permits consideration of other possible reasons for the staff's shying away from the workshops, such as the fear of being called racist, of not having concerns taken seriously, or of being accused of being too sensitive.

Stress Caused by Other Events in the Library Manifesting Itself as Resistance to Diversity

If the library experiences stress because of dwindling resources, staff cutbacks, and an increasingly needy patron population, it is difficult to assess what is truly resistance to working on diversity and what is reluctance to take on anything new. It is misguided to assume other stresses alone cause negative program evaluations, but it is also unwise not to take those concerns into account.

How Can a Useful System of Evaluation Be Established?

Three important factors in a useful evaluation process are that it is continual, it has both formal and informal aspects, and it is multifaceted.

Just as a plan for creating a multicultural environment defines an on-going process, the evaluation of various goals guiding that process must also be continuous. The initial climate assessment—ranging from doing initial staff interviews to examining the collection and programs already in place—provides a basis of information for later comparison. Periodic evaluation of staff attitudes, services, and materials are conducted in the same manner and measured against the earlier evaluations to determine the level of progress. One of the hardest parts about evaluation is having the discipline and time to do it.

Evaluation should be both formal and informal. Periodically, a formal survey should ask the staff where they see this effort going, what they see changing, and what additional tools and information they feel they need. Change in the collection can be similarly evaluated, formally asking the staff if they are adding to or altering their periodical subscription lists, if they are intentionally including materials that reflect diversity in their displays, and so on. Informally, information comes by talking with staff about their response to a recent film on racism or something in the news or by reading the graffiti in the bathrooms. While this information is difficult to quantify, it surely takes a snapshot of the changes occurring in the library.

A good evaluation process must also be multifaceted. Virtually everything done in moving toward valuing diversity should be noted and evaluated in some way. An evaluation of a film series considers both the viewers' responses to the chosen films *and* the experience of those responsible for putting the program together. An evaluation of staff training sessions analyzes how people felt about the sessions, what they learned, and how they will incorporate the experience into their daily work lives. A multifaceted evaluation of people's responses to such a session can be done formally or informally. While an evaluation of hiring changes—who is hired, what the recruiting process looks like, what kinds of questions are asked in the interviews—provides data directly relevant to the diversity process, an investigation of why people leave adds critical information as well. Exit interviews can obtain alternate perceptions of the organization's environment and activities.

The facts gathered in an evaluation process should be preserved in a fairly formal manner with one or two designated holders of the information. At least annually, a report compiling the data should be published and disseminated to staff, patrons, and other interested people. A public, annual report on the library's diversity efforts sends the message that the institution continues to be committed to creating an hospitable, multicultural environment and integrates the evaluation process into the work on diversity as a whole.

What Should Be Looked for and Not Looked for in the Evaluation Progress?

This final section on evaluation is about being realistic. Some things can be expected to show up in the data, such as changes in behavior of staff. If the staff, for example, is notorious for telling jokes based on race, gender, or sexual orientation, people's perceptions about the frequency of that phenomenon can be measured by asking how often they hear such jokes. The wider the variety of people, the more accurate the data; in every organization, some hear demeaning jokes, and some lack awareness or perceive them differently. Subtle changes in a person's approach to others are less measurable. However, it is possible to note differences in staff interactions—to whom they speak, with whom they socialize and eat, the tenor of meetings and work conversations—in the search for signs of a different feel in the environment, one that is more open and inclusive.

It is not realistic to expect miracles or an organizational cure. If an evaluation seeks proof of dramatic change and finds it, the chances are good that the wrong questions have been asked or the answers are misleading. For example, a white staff asked if people of color should be in the senior management of the organization will probably say yes, regardless of their beliefs. Instead, the fact of people of color in senior management positions and their treatment once there truly measures the staff's commitment to diversity, regardless of what they say they believe. Recruiting and hiring practices change slowly; evaluation should monitor that slow change process *and push it along* without expecting staff members to transform overnight to hire entirely differently than they ever have before. It is also unrealistic to expect that the evaluation process will, all by itself, bring about change. However, with formal and informal measures built into the long-range plan, evaluation can contribute to personal and institutional change.

To summarize, the evaluation process is an essential element in creating a multicultural environment. Because many factors complicate the evaluation of work on sensitive issues, it is important to be realistic in designing ways to assess the climate in and progress of an organization. To be most effective, evaluation should be continuous, formal and informal, and multifaceted. Evaluation can be used as a tool to educate staff members, to heighten their awareness, to encourage them to alter their behavior, and to measure the changes they make. The evaluation process, like change in an organization, is most effective when it is planned as opposed to happening randomly. Often, when unplanned, measurement occurs sporadically and in a scatter shot manner, limiting the information gleaned. For example, to know what employees think about their supervisors' support of the diversity program, they should be asked. To assess changes in those perceptions, the same (or similar) question should be asked at regular points in the long-range plan. There is no one way to evaluate progress in becoming a more hospitable environment, but the right way monitors changes with a thoughtful evaluation plan.

CONCLUSION

To fully serve its patrons and provide an hospitable workplace for its employees, a library must closely examine its collections, its hiring practices, its policies and procedures, its formal and informal rules, and the communication among staff members to be certain that there is support for diversity in each of these areas. While there is no one way to create an hospitable, multicultural environment in the library, there are elements of a successful transition to such a workplace, as well as identifiable steps in making changes in the organization's culture.

Creating a multicultural environment in the library is a lengthy, arduous task. As the people who work at the University of Michigan have discovered, it is an effort met with both enthusiasm and resistance. It is also an exciting and essential endeavor for every modern library.

7

The University
of Michigan Library's
Diversity Committee

Elaine Jordan

PURPOSE

The Library Diversity Committee (LDC) provides leadership to the staff by promoting understanding across racial and cultural lines as well as addressing the issues of gender and sexual orientation and the concerns of people with disabilities. It also acts as an advisory group to the library administration, reporting on diversity programs and staff and patron concerns. It leads into the creation and implementation of a range of diversity activities.

COMPOSITION

The committee at the University of Michigan consists of 12 members with the Manager of Personnel and Payroll Services and a representative of library administration serving as ex-officio members. The remaining 10 members are recruited from the staff at large for two-year staggered terms, five members leaving the committee each year. The *Library Newsletter* and other internal communication vehicles announce requests for new member nominations. Self-nominations are also accepted. The committee reviews the names and then submits candidates to the Dean of the University Library who appoints the five new members. Care is taken to maintain a diverse committee crossing job, racial, cultural, and gender lines. Vacancies occurring during the year are not filled. New members receive orientation packets containing the committee's charge and operating procedures, goals, minutes from past meetings, and articles on diversity issues.

Once a year, old and new members attend a team-building workshop, facilitated by an outside consultant who helps set the committee's ground rules and makes the members more comfortable in discussing often sensitive issues and opinions with each other. Throughout the year, the committee attends evaluation workshops to assess actions, focus on its goals, and work on additional projects.

ROLE OF MEMBERS

Committee members keep abreast of and actively participate in diversity activities. In program implementation, they often serve as planners, facilitators, or discussion group leaders—a role that requires sensitivity to all staff. Members have the responsibility to keep people talking about diversity issues in their individual units and in small discussion groups. Members encourage the staff to speak with them, on a one-to-one basis if necessary, to bring suggestions, concerns, and problems related to multiculturalism to the committee.

Rules and Process

1. Set meeting place and time.
The committee should meet at a regularly scheduled time—at least once a month—and at a conveniently located place. A round table allows eye contact and gives everyone a sense of equality. Comfortable chairs help everyone relax. The environment should feel safe, allowing and encouraging free, open discussions.

2. Rotate chairpersons and recorders periodically.

A chairperson and a recorder conduct each meeting. Committee members may rotate these positions according to the membership roster. A rotating chair allows everyone an opportunity to share power, set the agenda, and conduct the meetings, thereby creating a sense, if not a reality, of equal sharing of responsibilities. It also gives the group a chance to experience different leadership styles.

3. Develop a sense of confidentiality, commitment, and trust.

Members must commit to the ultimate goal of the committee to eradicate social oppression in all forms. Multicultural issues are often sensitive and, even in the most committed group, lead to heated discussions. While members are expected to be sensitive to all cultural or social groups represented on the committee, established rules of confidentiality allow committee members to feel free to voice their opinions and feelings during meetings.

4. Establish channels for on-going communication.

Campus mail works well for the regular exchange of articles on diversity issues. Electronic mail provides an efficient method for disseminating more important updates and urgent messages. The library's newsletter publicizes the committee activities, and fliers notify staff of upcoming events. Mounted public displays and exhibits call attention to library resources on gender, race, and ethnic studies.

5. Establish a budget to handle expenses.

The committee agrees on a workable budget which includes estimates for speakers' costs, equipment and room rentals, travel expenses, refreshments, etc. before submitting it to the administration for approval. Additional monies required for special events or programs may also be solicited from other departments in the University, surrounding communities, local businesses, grant organizations, and foundations.

6. Organize program implementation.

At Michigan, one organizational approach to program implementation formed external and internal subcommittees within the diversity committee. The external subcommittees handle staff involvement programs such as the Amity Program, film serials, exhibits, mentoring, etc. and include committee members and staff. These subcommittees allow the staff a chance to plan diversity activities and encourage teamwork among themselves and committee members. By involving as many people as possible, diversity efforts receive broader support. Internal subcommittees manage diversity committee activities such as publicity and long range planning.

PROGRAMS AND ACTIVITIES

A variety of programs and activities provide an opportunity for staff to learn about diversity issues. The diversity committee encourages and assists staff development of suggestions for programs. The committee includes in its discussions all ideas for diversity programs and activities suggested by the administration and staff. Some ideas get referred to the appropriate department in the library (e.g., personnel, staff development). Others get planned and executed by an external subcommittee or a volunteer staff group.

Interaction among the committee, staff groups, and departments requires open lines of communication and reduced duplication of diversity efforts. Communication improves when 1) at least one committee member serves on each staff planning group and reports back to the diversity committee, or 2) group chairpersons and department planners periodically report to the committee.

AMITY PROGRAM

The library's Amity Program creates a warm, welcoming, and inviting environment for new employees as they enter into a large, diverse community. Existing staff members volunteer, on an informal basis, to meet and help ease new employees into the social and professional life of the university and the local community.

The Amity Committee organizes the program and writes guidelines for volunteers and letters of welcome to new library staff members. Its five to ten volunteer staff members meet one-to-one with new staff for a period of up to six months. Meetings typically occur during breaks and lunches, although the interaction is strictly up to the volunteer and the new staff member. Volunteers also accompany newcomers to meetings and introduce them to other staff members. Additional pairings are made as new staff arrive. The program encourages group lunches with several new staff and a volunteer, continuing one-to-one matches when requested and hosting twice-a-year teas and receptions to introduce new staff.

Tips for an Amity Program

1. A staff-driven committee better assesses the need for a friendlier environment.
2. Evaluate success of each event and be ready to change, if necessary (e.g., if one-to-one matches do not always work, try group lunches).
3. Seek secretarial support to send letters, make matches, do publicity, etc.
4. Establish a budget for refreshments, publicity, and other necessary items.

DISCUSSION GROUPS

After UM held a program entitled "Overcoming Racism: Exploring the Value of Diversity" in April 1988, staff members formed discussion groups, with 8 to 12 participants in each, to continue to talk about their attitudes toward race and racism. The library administration approved release time to attend discussion sessions. Members of the Diversity Committee facilitated each group, arranged meeting times and places, and reported on the groups' activities. Without abandoning issues of race, discussions expanded to include a variety of topics, such as:

- Recruitment of a diversified workforce,
- Staff performance evaluations,
- Library exhibits,
- Ethnic humor,

- Newspaper and magazine articles on diversity issues,
- Grievances,
- Standard and non-standard English,
- Job retention, and
- Affirmative action.

Small discussion groups produced frank conversations about sensitive issues and the open expression of personal feelings concerning diversity in the library. Discussions widened to address issues of gender and sexual orientation in the broader context of human relations. Many diversity programs such as the exhibits, film series, Amity Program, as well as some staff development programs, grew out of these original discussion groups.

EXHIBITS

Diversity-related exhibits prove that the library welcomes many cultures and philosophies and permits a lively, artistic, informative presentation of diversity issues. Branch libraries can use exhibits to promote the diversity in their fields of specialty if desired. For example, UM's Fine Arts Library mounted an exhibit entitled, "People of Color in the History of Art." Other previous exhibits at University of Michigan Library include the following:

- "The Rulers of Africa,"
- "Paintings and Sculptures by African-American Artists,"
- "Diversity Through Literature,"
- "African-Americans in American Culture,"
- "The History of African-American Women in Nursing," and
- "African-American Musicians."

FILM SERIES

Films and videos not only educate through entertainment but also inspire lively follow-up discussions. When properly selected, they are useful tools for experienced and inexperienced programmers alike. Films and videos provide information, stimulate thought and discussion, arouse emotions, generate understanding, and confront subjects otherwise too sensitive or difficult to broach. As a vicarious medium, they can transport viewers to another time, another place, another culture.

Films and videos work best in a group setting. Proper introduction places the film or video in context and focuses the audience's attention on the issues at hand. Post-discussions and other activities reinforce learning. Committee members or experts on the film's subject matter can do the introduction and lead the discussion. For example, when showing the film "Long Time Companion," someone with expertise in gay and lesbian issues or AIDS might lead the discussion.

Materials Planning and Selection

After careful preview, committee members select films and videos for diversity film festivals and special events. Previewing responsibly ensures the selection of only the best materials and prepares program leaders for the promotion, screening, and discussing of the films.

Materials, rooms, equipment, and technical crew should be scheduled as far in advance as possible. Rooms for showing films must be checked for sufficient darkening, unobstructed screen visibility, and equipment readiness. Projection equipment should be tested in the room and checked for compatibility with the film or video:

- 16mm film requires a 16mm projector with optical sound,
- 3/4 inch U-matic videocassettes need a 3/4 inch video deck for playback, and
- 1/2 inch videocassettes, such as those found in a video store, need a 1/2 inch video playback deck.

If showing a tape from overseas, make sure that it is NTSC standard so that it is compatible with U.S. equipment. Some video players, especially 3/4 inch players, have a built-in switch for PAL—the other standard often used overseas. Video stores with large immigrant clientele may also rent PAL players.

If the expected audience is 25 or fewer people, a large TV monitor will probably be adequate for showing. Larger audiences need a video projector enlarging the image to several feet across, or a ratio of one monitor per 25 people. Enough time should be allowed to set up, focus, and troubleshoot the equipment prior to show time.

Film Rental and References

Numerous options exist for film rental, including the following:

1. Local public libraries often offer film and video materials for free or minimal costs.
2. The University of Michigan Film and Video Library can rent most film and video titles to off-campus groups nationwide. Materials can be reserved up to 15 months in advance. Customers can request a listing of its holdings on diversity-related or multicultural topics by writing to

> Film and Video Library
> The University of Michigan
> Room 207 Undergraduate Library
> 919 South University Avenue
> Ann Arbor, MI 48109-1185
> Phone: (313) 764-5360
>   (800) 999-0424

3. Other university libraries rent films. "Educational Film and Video Locator," published by Bowker, lists the holdings of libraries that are members of the Consortium of College and University Media Centers. Materials rented from university libraries cost considerably less than those rented from commercial distributors.
4. Commercial distributors can be located through *The Video Source Book* and the third edition of *Film and Video Finder* (Medford, NJ: National Information Center for Educational Media, a Division of Access Innovation, Inc., 1991).
5. For inquiries on a specific title or distributor not found in one of the printed reference works,
   a) contact the reference librarian at a local film/video library,
   b) call the UM Film and Video Library for reference assistance, or

c) fax an information request to the American Film and Video Association Service at (800) 354-1449. First inquiry is free.

COPYRIGHT ISSUES

Program presenters must consider the provisions of the copyright law when contemplating the exhibition of materials for which they do not have public performance rights, such as video copies of feature films that have been released theatrically. Users should be very conservative in their interpretation of "fair-use" provisions of the Copyright Law, Title 17 of the United States Code.

MENTORING

Mentoring supports the Library's goals for recruitment and retention of people of color as well as general staff development. UM's Amity Committee outlined a team mentoring approach, in which a competent peer with strong interpersonal skills meets regularly over a significant period of time with a small group of new staff having similar job functions. Mentoring provides a confidential forum for questions, concerns, issues, and needs of a personal and professional nature and builds a library-wide network of staff with contacts in departments beyond their own immediate area.

The inclusion of mentors of color has a positive effect on both the mentor and the new staff member. New employees see the mentor as knowledgeable, valuable members of the organization. People of color may see them as role models with whom they can identify and perhaps have some commonalities. Because racism is built into organizations, mentors of color may reduce perceived racial intent in supervisor comments, in co-worker interaction, or in the mentoring process itself. A mentoring program not only creates a welcoming atmosphere in the library but also produces other identifiable benefits:

- A positive welcoming experience that continues through the first crucial months of employment;

- A recruitment tool with which to convince potential candidates that the entire library system is committed to their professional growth and personal satisfaction in the work environment;
- A developed cadre of mentors who can assist staff with developing new skills; and
- A general improvement in staff morale.

Several issues worth considering for a team mentoring program are

- How are mentors identified?
- How large should the groups be?
- What time frames are appropriate in terms of meetings and contacting new employees?
- How should groups be organized?
- What framework should be provided for the group discussions?
- Should the first meeting be a routine part of training?
- Will group mentoring preclude the need for individual mentoring?

ISSUES IN INVOLVEMENT AND COMMITMENT

The first step is gaining staff involvement and buy-in. A diversity committee, like other library committees, does not work in isolation. To do so would diminish its effectiveness and value to the library. The committee must avoid being viewed as the group in charge of diversity issues for the library and the presumption that the other staff has no real role in and, hence, no real responsibility for diversity. The committee must gain the support, the involvement, and the commitment of other staff. As with most efforts, this is easier said than done. Clearly, the various activities sponsored and promoted by the committee can foster consideration of the issues related to diversity and multiculturalism in the library. Discussion groups also promote staff involvement.

Discussion groups at Michigan began as an offshoot of early training sessions for the entire staff. An unexpected benefit arose as many of these groups continued to informally meet and discuss diversity, sharing their experiences and viewpoints on various aspects. Members of the groups often enlisted their colleagues to join and, occasionally, to lead the discussion groups, widening the circle of those concerned enough about topics to devote their lunch hours to examining them. More importantly, the staff, through no extra University efforts, recognized that all people, those different and alike, could make valuable contributions to the library, the university, and the community.

Another step involved the establishment of subcommittees of library staff to work on specific projects such as exhibits. Future plans include opening some committee meetings to the staff at large and meeting with focus groups of staff in various work areas.

The administration takes the lead in clearly defining the benefits of multiculturalism to the library, its staff, users, and quality of service. Buy-ins are rarely achieved on the basis of a higher good. Individuals often need to see a direct benefit to themselves before accepting the premise of the value of a diverse and multicultural workplace.

Patrons of diverse cultures clearly benefit when the staff meets their needs and is as helpful to them as to the majority clientele. Hiring and retaining a multicultural staff reduces bias in service, as well as bias in the collection. An environment hospitable to all staff is equally hospitable to patrons. The minimum workplace standard should expect no less.

My Issue's Better Than Yours

A diversity committee represents, and acts as a microcosm of, the larger staff when the committee's make-up reflects the different racial, ethnic, religious, and sexual orientation backgrounds of the staff at large. Individuals bring to the group the same concerns, prejudices, "isms," fears, and group loyalties held before becoming members of the committee. This often creates divisions within the committee, mirroring the divisions within the organization and society: Latinos versus Anglos in the Southwest; Native Americans versus Caucasians in the Northwest; African-Americans versus Asians and Arabs versus Jews in the

East; African-Americans versus Caucasians in the South or Mid-west; and women versus men everywhere. To work effectively, committee members must manage the diversity on the diversity committee.

At Michigan, the diversity of the committee members surfaces in frank and occasionally painful discussions. Decisions often result from consensus rather than unanimity. Committee members must remember why the committee exists and strive to achieve the goals they set for the committee and the organization, regardless of individual differences.

Committees Are People Too

Issues in valuing diversity and multiculturalism are not easy to tackle. They involve deeply held beliefs and strong emotions. The fact that these people want to get involved and serve on diversity committees usually indicates a greater openness and willingness to learn than may be true of other staff. It also makes them more vulnerable to the discomfort that comes with tackling difficult issues. Individual passions naturally bubble over when held so constantly close to such heated issues. Committee members must find ways to deal with their own feelings in a positive manner.

At Michigan, a variety of approaches have been taken. Periodic retreats with an outside consultant as a facilitator have proven beneficial in that the uncomfortable topics do get discussed, and each member gains insight into one's own feelings. Another recently adopted tactic established informal, monthly lunches for the committee members, permitting the members to relax and relate to one another simply as colleagues without the pressures of dealing with a specific agenda.

GLACIERS DO MOVE

Attitudes and behaviors do not change quickly. The issues discussed today—racism, sexism, and homophobia—were discussed twenty years ago, one hundred years ago, four hundred years ago in this country. They have been issues, whether discussed or not, in most civilizations, cultures, and eras and ages. The efforts of a diversity committee will make only a small difference, causing it frustration, burn-out, and occasional feelings of failure and despair. A sense of purpose and concrete, achievable goals prevents such feelings and permits a sense of accomplishment.

The goal of the library and its diversity committee may be, eventually, to change attitudes; but, this goal is intangible, unmeasurable and, ultimately, entirely up to individuals, not the committee. The committee and the library should instead strive for changes in behavior that produce measurable, tangible results, eliminating behaviors that inhibit the ability to work effectively, the environment's hospitality, or the quality of patron service.

IMPACT AND RESULTS

The UM Library raises consciousness on issues of diversity through numerous efforts: diversity film festivals, the Amity Committee, and multicultural exhibits and speakers sponsored by the diversity committee. Multicultural activities increase understanding and empathy between minorities and the majority group within the library. Further, the committee gives valuable input on hiring decisions for administrators, the diversity librarian, and the coordinator of Academic Outreach Services.

It also serves as a forum to debate diversity issues in relation to administration. Diversity and multiculturalism are not just moral imperatives; they are a sound investment for any organization. As a microcosm of the staff at large, the committee ensures that the voices of all groups are heard before policy is set, molding the policies with positive pressure. With a diversity committee bridging communication between the staff and administration, no matter what policies are ultimately set, staff from all groups can rest assured that they played a part in the process.

8

Cultural Diversity Staff Development Activities: What's in it for Me?

Maurice B. Wheeler

SETTING THE STAGE

Despite the recent attention given to cultural diversity, particularly since the mid-1980s, comparatively little change has actually occurred. The number of people of color in formerly all white organizations has increased as the nation has been dragged, kicking and screaming, into the age of affirmative action. Still, few organizational cultures actively encourage retention or acknowledge the value of difference. The problems of racism, bigotry, prejudice, and insensitivity have not yielded to the usual interventions, and the problems of functioning in a pluralistic society remain with us. The tenor of the Reagan and Bush administrations has enabled many people to express openly their disregard for social, economic, and educational efforts to achieve parity in this society. Often people ignore or tolerate discrimination or prejudice until it affects them directly, until an experience causes a change in their perceptions.

The effective management of a culturally diverse workforce will become a business and service imperative for every successful organization of the future. Librarians striving to make their organizations serve students of every ethnic, social, and religious culture on a daily basis must reframe their approach to staffing and services. As many academic library directors and deans chose to act upon this imperative before the parent institution issues an administrative mandate, their groundbreaking steps may be taken without the benefit of experienced guidance. Although this chapter primarily focuses on the development of workshops, it discusses the full range of conditions that must be in place to make the workshops effective.

Management sends a strong message of commitment early in the process and positions the effort for success through two administrative actions: the appointment of a manager to be in charge of the change process; and the establishment of an adequate budget. The manager should be a respected person of power, influence, and integrity, as this person, along with the director and top administrators, sets the tone of the process. Much effort must be made to ensure that the change process is seen not as the domain of the change agent or manager alone, but as the responsibility of every member of the staff.

DEFINING ORGANIZATIONAL PHILOSOPHY

Achieving cultural diversity is undoubtedly one of the most difficult organizational changes facing library directors today. In designating diversity as an area of focus, the director must establish a clear and consistent message of organizational and administrative commitment. Staff should not be led to believe that cultural diversity occurs with one awareness or sensitivity workshop. Only through many experiences and events do cultural attitudes within an organization move from sensitivity through tolerance, acceptance, and beyond. Increasing the number of people of color on the staff does not achieve plurality; it simply increases representation. Equity of power, opportunity, and influence must be an important part of the organizational philosophy and aim.

At the outset, everyone in the organization must know that diversity is not a crusade, neither personal nor organizational. In support of that approach, a written philosophy statement should be drafted and used during the planning process. The case for diversity must be stated in terms of business rationales linked directly to library users, services, performance, and methods of operation. A competitive stance in the increasingly global arena of the information profession, diverse talent pools, and the dividends from complete staff cultivation are but a few points with which to build the business case.

The library must willingly endure severe systemic change and great organizational discomfort to advance in multiculturalism. The effort must always be portrayed as long-term and strategic and requiring major changes in the way people think and act in relation to cultural diversity.

Even if a library already has a diverse workforce, that diversity creates many issues that beg to be addressed. Treating everyone in a diverse workforce the same does not equal workforce diversity. All people are not the same; it is foolish to pretend they are.

ESTABLISH SCOPE AND PURPOSE

In some libraries, particularly a few academic libraries, staff development activities relating to cultural diversity progress quickly beyond tuition reimbursement and special events programming to strategic training and developmental activities. As women and people of color become less receptive to a behavior model of assimilation, administrators and staff development officers must provide staff with more skills necessary to work effectively in their environment. Affirmative action, even with its merits, addresses only the symptoms of individual and institutional racism, focusing on the how instead of the why people of color and women have not been hired and retained and have not traditionally held positions of power and influence. Established convictions become questionable when approached from a different perspective. Thus, awareness building activities successfully bring diversity issues to the forefront and initiate the dialogue that precedes systemic cultural change.

An organization must absolutely and clearly articulate the purpose of its activities and the scope of the tasks to be accomplished. Such articulation requires, at least, a basic understanding of the dynamics of multicultural and gender training. A simple and uncomplicated approach often works best, starting, for instance, with a discussion on a broad-based subject: how to set the stage for greater personal and organizational development or how to eliminate entrenched social and organizational habits. Other more narrowly focused topics to be addressed in awareness building activities include racism, differences in communication styles, interpersonal discrimination and prejudice, systemic barriers, beliefs and attitudes, dominant culture characteristics, and stereotypes. These discussions must also give the participants the necessary knowledge and skills to deal with the experience afterwards. In initiating a long-term process, the participants should expect a feeling of having unfinished business. They must also expect the experience to disquiet some who, therefore, will not respond positively. Fear of change and anxiety inevitably come as part of the change process.

ESTABLISH ATTENDANCE REQUIREMENTS: VOLUNTARY VS. MANDATORY

There are strong arguments on both sides of the issue of attendance. More programs succeed, however, when workshop participation is required. Many reasons exist why a staff person might choose not to attend or might not encourage the staff to attend. Many people simply do not see a problem with racism, and therefore, feel efforts on the topic waste time and money. Others waver, torn between responding to the issue and the productivity concerns of their department. Yet, others resist because they find their belief systems very comfortable and have no desire to have an outsider come in to suggest that they might have some racist or exclusionary attitudes. However, not everyone who would rather be somewhere else intends a negative reflection on the subject matter. Many staff members resist because the presentation of the issues have borne no immediate relevancy for them. Others may consider it basic or trivial. Still others, because of some involvement in the civil rights movement of the 1960s, vehemently resist any suggestion that they, too, might have racial issues to address. A strong argument supporting mandatory attendance says that staff members need a common vocabulary and philosophical awareness. Workshops equally inform everyone about the library's commitment to the issue and its expectation of them as employees. Mandatory attendance also significantly adds to the critical mass of people needed to actually cause change in the organization.

Complete systemic change requires a significant commitment of resources. In light of that commitment, the library administration can hardly justify a come-if-you-want approach. In such cases, attendance will likely be "strongly encouraged." This kind of language often sounds as a call to duty anyway, prompting many to actually attend without being officially mandated. In fact, those staff members may have perceived the wording as a cowardly administration's poorly articulated attempt to mandate attendance, making them feel pushed into it anyway.

A voluntary attendance policy results in a wide variation among unit participation. Initially, there is usually no consistent commitment on the part of units and managers. Without the total commitment of the organization, especially those in managerial positions, the staff undoubtedly receives contradictory messages about the importance of the awareness raising process.

GETTING STARTED

An important part of getting started is to find out who has already engaged in this kind of activity, what their methods were, and if they are willing to offer assistance. As is the case on many large campuses, several units might engage in the same type of staff development activities without the others' knowledge. Identifying resources on a local, regional, and national level proves to be an exercise well worth the effort. Surveying existing programs at other institutions gains much insight useful when assessing the suitability of a consultant and their method of delivery.

Select Consultants and Trainers

As the complexity of the racial problems in our society become more apparent, many consultants will join those already providing training in this area. Unfortunately, not all of them are equally effective, even in the most controlled setting.

The first step is to find consultants who can model the image envisioned for the organization. A single consultant joins with a training partner to create a diverse team. A team mixed by race and gender helps mirror a positive and inclusive image to the staff. The consultants must analyze and understand the library's organizational culture to choose appropriate interventions and methods of delivery, and yet must have the flexibility and perceptiveness to know when to make adjustments to accommodate the environment. Consultants must also model appropriate behavior. As their behavior has a powerful effect on the outcome of the training, they should, at all times, be in harmony with the spirit of the program. The consultants' behavior should never erode anyone's self-esteem; they must resist the urge to engage in battle when provoked. Disruption and inaction must be confronted, while remaining focused on behavior rather than personality or attitude, sticking steadfastly to the agenda. Workshops require a motivating and participatory climate, balancing accommodation and education. Consultants must be able to manage conflict, as when a disruptive participant deflects the topic. Lastly, they should not be afraid to identify, definitively, right and wrong behavior. The toleration of racist or sexist views and behavior runs counter to the purpose of hiring a consultant.

Consultants are the facilitators of, not the key to, the change effort. When the partnership between consultant and organization does not work, the consultant, not the commitment to change, should be terminated. It is important, however, to be certain the problem lies with the consultant and not with the system. It takes much knowledge and experience to move an organization forward, while serving as a scapegoat at the same time.

Establish and Review a Budget

Often, the person managing the project—the change-agent—lacks a framework for formulating and justifying a realistic budget for such a project. Most organizations succeeding in this area have been corporations with millions of dollars at their disposal for special projects. A few academic models exist, but all libraries present different sets of circumstances, making the approximate cost to get the job done difficult to determine. A well-planned budget considers several questions:

- Is the library's change-agent adequately equipped to lead this effort?
- Are additional informational and instructional materials needed?
- Is additional training required?
- What are the costs?
- Will the consultants and trainers be local, regional, or national in scope?
- Is it necessary to have a consultant of national reputation to achieve success?.
- Will a general budget absorb operational costs such as support staff, supplies, equipment, telecommunications, and other miscellaneous costs?
- Are there financial implications in taking staff from their normal responsibilities to attend the workshops?
- Will a separate budget line cover the consultants' fees and expenses and other workshop related costs?

Regardless of which consultants are selected and what methods of intervention are used, the effort must receive adequate resources. Financial resources alone cannot ensure success, but inadequate funding will surely hobble the project. Resources set aside in special budget lines launch the associated efforts. Additionally, these funds must remain in place throughout the transitional period and for however long it takes to sustain the effects of the change.

Determine Program and Workshop Format

After clearly articulated goals and objectives have been established, the next most important task is to determine the appropriate methods for achieving the desired results. When library administrators plan strategically for the next period, they do so from a strong base of experience and knowledge. Planning cultural diversity activities requires the same approach. Even when a consultant suggests appropriate methods of training, library administrators should function from a common knowledge base. This base might best evolve by having the top administrators participate in a two or three day retreat on organizational culture, race, and gender issues prior to large-scale planning. Selecting a few "isms" and exploring them deeply is preferable to including every kind of "ism" and bigotry. An in-depth approach to the issues of race and gender foments tremendous personal growth, transferrable to other issues of prejudice and bigotry.

The library administration must ensure that the staff has a clear understanding of its objectives and that they take those objectives as their own. Identified need forms the basis of objectives. If the staff does not see the need as valid, they surely will not see merit in the exploration of a solution for those needs. For the process to be most effective, the staff must cooperate during the presentation. They must know what is going to happen and what is expected of them as participants.

Above all, learning depends upon having an environment that is open and safe for self-revelation. Careful configuration of workshop groups prevents initial barriers created by drastic differences in organizational rank and status. Such disparity in the beginning stage causes the lower level staff to fear that they are taking a great risk and the higher level to fear being mis-quoted or taken out of context. Confidentiality cannot be stressed enough. Combining it with respect and tact forms the ground rule for all training sessions. The learning process must permit rough edges. Everyone must be comfortable expressing ideas and fully developing thoughts. Best results occur when the workshop participants are arranged focusing on key groups in the library: people of color, white men, supervisors, and top administrators.

The initial training should be presented in two or three day workshops for groups of 10 or less, depending upon the flexibility of the library and the number of people to be trained. In larger groups, non-talkers often feel intimidated. Smaller groups permit each participant to have a greater sense of self-commitment and allow no one to hide from the issues being discussed.

Although the training should be customized specifically for an organization, some basics should be covered. Workshop structures should give the participants sufficient time to move into a learning mode and address the following issues:

- The stereotypes of racism and sexism.
- How stereotypes effect their daily lives and organization.
- Alternative behaviors.
- Development of personal and organizational change guidelines pertaining to their spheres of influence.

Whether the change effort begins with a one-day workshop or a comprehensive series to train all employees-executives, managers, line employees, and support staff, a variety of interventions can be used effectively. If this is not the organization's first attempt at diversity activities, additional factors merit consideration when choosing the program content. A secondary session often entails more difficulty, particularly if the initial session was either inappropriate or incomplete. Diversity training that does not allow an in-depth exploration of the core of a person's racism, bigotry, and insensitivity often only serves to make the person smarter in their racist behavior.

Determine Site Selection

The site must allow the staff to deal with these issues without the disruption of their normal daily routines. A complete change of setting must be provided. The setting needs to be pleasant and as accommodating as possible to avoid distractions, atmospheric or environmental. Where time and financial resources will permit, an off-campus retreat gives staff the time and space to really explore their personal feelings without the mental interruptions of daily life: traffic, meals, children, and myriad other daily encounters that shift their focus and drain their energy.

Details, Details, Details

Inattention to the numerous details involved in arranging a workshop can severely tarnish the effect of an otherwise well planned and effective activity. To keep the outcome from becoming tainted by neglected details, the organizer must plan ahead and prepare to handle swiftly, and with confidence, anything that might go wrong.

The details involved vary from one place to the next; however, the following are a few considerations to keep in mind.

1. Room arrangement. A formal room arrangement—formal rows of chairs, a podium or raised platform, etc.—usually suggests a lecture and focuses the attention solely on the facilitator, thus inhibiting free-flowing exchange. Participants often feel put in the spotlight whenever asked to talk, as the focus shifts from the presenter to them. Any kind of barrier between the facilitator and the participants detrimentally effects the discourse. The environment should be relaxed, with easily rearranged, comfortable chairs, and any central focus created by physical properties eliminated.

An out-of-the-way area of the room should be stocked with ready refreshments: coffee and assorted beverages along with energizing morning and afternoon snacks.

2. Equipment. The facilitators' equipment requests must be known well in advance and reserved with the hosting facility. Plans should be made to have the equipment set up and tested by the hosting facility or rental agency prior to the start of each session. The usual requests include a video player and monitor, an overhead projector and screen, and easels with paper and colored markers.

3. Workshop materials. Far in advance of the workshop date, the facilitator should provide the contact person with a copy of the materials to be used. If the host institution is to provide participants with copies of handouts, explicit instructions need to be given regarding their duplication and arrangement. Any other miscellaneous needs must also be conveyed as early as possible.

4. Accommodations for consultants. Travel typically includes round trip transportation to and from the point of departure. Accommodation details include hotel reservations, form of payment, and meal arrangements. Hospitality includes getting the facilitator to and from the workshop site. Lastly, at least two questions regarding compensation should be addressed prior to the consultant's arrival:

1. Is preparation time included in the workshop fee?
2. Is payment required immediately upon completion of workshop?

Promotion and Advertisement

Mandatory workshop attendance virtually nullifies promotion and advertisement. However, the staff must have, at least, the correct logistical information. Last minute changes cause confusion. The date, place, and time should be set in stone before disseminating that information. Staff can be notified of further important details in many ways. Personal letters from a top administrator, preferably the dean or director, always make a strong impact. It can come either in the form of an invitation or as a reminder, if attendance is required. A flyer or brief announcement in the staff newsletter or similar publications also serves as a tickler.

If possible, some effort should be made to inform the campus of the library's programming in the area of cultural diversity. Other units on campus should know that there are resource people available in the library.

Methods of Evaluation

There are many methods to evaluate the actual workshops. Usually, a standard form—eliciting the staff members' expectations, their opinion of what they learned and what should be improved upon or changed, and an assessment of the facilitator's effectiveness—produces useful information. When evaluating workshops dealing with sensitive subjects, a word of caution is appropriate. If attendance is required, a significant number of evaluations will be negative. Some staff will take this as an opportunity to express the displeasure they were reluctant to show during the workshop. Unfortunately, this leaves the facilitator without an opportunity to address these comments in an open forum. Others uncomfortable expressing their disdain with the issue of racism and other "isms" usually expend much time and energy elaborating on the faults of the program design, method of presentation, and the facilitator. Many of these comments, although presented with anger, contain valid points worthy of consideration, instead of completely dismissing them as the rantings of diehard racists.

In addition to the evaluation immediately following the

workshops, a follow-up sent to participants several weeks later culls additional perspectives that evolve as time permits the staff members to more fully process the information in a less emotional setting.

Of equal or even greater importance are evaluations of the workshops' long-term effectiveness. The overall administrative plan should include these mechanisms with an indication of who is responsible for future initiatives.

PITFALLS

Take Care of the Change Agent

A multitude of things to consider arise in both preparing the system for change and maintaining that change. The role of the change agent is critical, and the organization must ensure the health of the person serving in that position. To prevent setting up oneself for sacrifice, the change agent must check for what have become known as "pockets of readiness." If there are none, one must determine if the timing of the effort is right. Systemic change cannot be accomplished alone. The change agent needs as much assistance as possible; offers of help should not be ignored. The lone crusader will not survive. As time passes, even the most stubborn will realize the task is far too enormous for any one person to be possessive of the process. Other staff members must be allowed and encouraged to also invest their time and energy. However, an individual's change does not translate to organizational change; the task will not become easier simply because a few individuals have joined the effort.

Just as the organization has to position itself for strategic planning on this issue, the change agent must also have a personal strategy to attempt only manageable tasks. While success requires planning, the approach must not become too conservative so as to limit the results. Many experienced consultants agree that the most important requirement is to stay healthy, both physically and emotionally. The change agent should not hesitate to take personal recovery time, especially after active involvement in facilitating training sessions. Organizational change requires many long hours and many frustrating periods. However, much frustration and anxiety can be prevented by acknowledging early in the process that things will seem to get worse before they get better. Often, the middle of the change effort looks and feels like failure.

Don't Ignore the Majority

Fear and anxiety are an accepted part of change. However, these reactions heightened when people lose sight of their place in the new environment. Each staff member must have an equal opportunity to learn about and contribute to the change.

After years of evaluating the successes and failures of cultural diversity training, sociologists have been led to ask a provocative question. Have white men been alienated and embittered in society's attempt to erase past inequities toward people of color and women? Indeed, white men have not been made to feel that they are equal partners in the change process. Many people who fear minimizing the atrocity of racism suggest that white men feel left out because they have been startled into the realization that they may not be able to achieve as much as their fathers, or at least not by utilizing the same methods.

In this era of heightened awareness of cultural diversity overshadowed by economic difficulty, it should not be surprising that there is defensiveness, concern, and backlash from white men. However, this effort cannot be accomplished without the participation of everyone. We must find a way to ensure that the change effort is a shared vision of everyone in the organization. White men are still the primary possessors of power in American society and in most of our organizations, either directly or indirectly. If they are not a partner in the change effort, a true systemic cultural change is virtually impossible.

WORKSHOP DESCRIPTION

The University of Michigan Library has made it possible for the staff to attend diversity-related workshops. Examples of them follow.

Title:
CROSS-CULTURAL COMMUNICATION WORKSHOP I

Description:
Presented by the program director of the International Center, this 1.5 hour program uses incidents that have occurred in the University of Michigan Library as a springboard for discussion and change. This workshop is open to any staff member, but is targeted specifically for those who work at public service desks. Student assistants are strongly encouraged to attend.

Objectives:
To reduce ethnocentrism, introduce participants to difficulties in cross-cultural communication, present strategies for effective communication, and briefly introduce elements of American culture that affect communication.

Title:
CROSS-CULTURAL COMMUNICATION WORKSHOPS II

Description:
Open to library staff who participated in the first half of the workshop, these four-hour workshops continue sensitizing and skill-building on the issues of ethnocentrism, the difficulties inherent in cross-cultural communication, the elements of American majority culture which affect communication, and present strategies for effective communication. Presented by the program director of the International Center.

Objectives:
Intermediate workshops—focus will be on interpersonal communication, discussing different styles and strategies for communicating with foreigners from cultures unfamiliar to the staff.

Advanced workshop—highly interactive, including a simulation designed to give the effect of visiting another culture, focuses on American majority culture and how majority American cultural values affect communication with minorities and people from other countries.

Title:
DEALING WITH FOREIGN STUDENTS

Description:
Although concerned with meeting the needs of a varied clientele, American library staffs are usually ill-equipped to deal with problems confronting foreign students. The large vocal population of native English speakers often eclipses the less aggressive foreign students. Cultural and linguistic barriers present added strains for an already busy staff. This two-hour workshop provides an opportunity to explore factors that contribute to differences in services provided to foreign students.

Objectives:
To teach staff to differentiate between cultural and individual behavior patterns, heighten their sensitivity to problems facing foreign students, and learn to communicate more effectively with the foreign student population.

Title:
DIVERSITY IN PRACTICE: CREATING A POSITIVE WORK ENVIRONMENT FOR GAY AND LESBIAN STAFF

Description:
A 3.5 hour workshop presented by a nationally recognized expert on sexual orientation issues to explore the barriers, conscious and unconscious, to gay and lesbian staff. Open to all Library staff, the topics to be covered include gay and lesbian staff as an invisible minority, the right to privacy vs. the need for recognition, employment contract provisions and health benefits, and relating personally on the job.

Objectives:
To explore the invisible barriers gay and lesbian staff may encounter and what may be done to remove or minimize these barriers.

Title:
AN EBONY VIEW OF THE IVORY TOWER:
A PROGRAM FOR PEOPLE OF COLOR

Description:
Open to all staff, especially staff of color, and presented by an organizational consultant with extensive experience in higher education, this 3.5 hour workshop examines certain fundamental cultural values of American institutions and organizations—the values of the white/Anglo North American mainstream. This system has worked successfully for the many people who make up the workforce—those who grew up with white/Anglo, primarily male, mainstream values, communication habits, and ways of thinking. Staff who come from different cultural backgrounds, communication patterns, and values may find it more difficult to fit in, understand the unwritten rules, and be successful in organizations—issues this workshop addresses.

Objectives:
To allow people of color to explore some mainstream cultural and work norms; identify barriers to success; discuss the importance of developing networks when left out of other networks; discuss coping strategies for dealing with isolation and lack of understanding, support, and positive feedback; become aware of the significance of the political fabric of the University of Michigan; and develop problem solving skills and strategies for success in this institution.

Title:
MANAGING A CULTURALLY DIVERSE WORKFORCE

Description:
A day-long workshop to present to supervisors of a multicultural workforce the special skills and sensibilities both to manage people who are different from themselves and to function effectively as part of a diverse team. Presented by a consultant on diversity issues, in this workshop supervisors of library staff will look at how their own biases, perceptions, and expectations about work affect managing others; examine what

it means to manage a diverse work place; and identify work styles and explore how they might be related to culture. The workshop will also help answer questions, such as how to recruit and retain people who are different from most of the people supervisors manage and how to evaluate and mentor people who are different from the majority of employees.

Objectives:
To help all supervisors of regular staffs to identify the special needs and additional skills they have in managing and how to acquire them.

Title:
RECRUITING AND RETAINING
A DIVERSIFIED WORKFORCE

Description:
A 2.5 hour workshop for all library supervisory staff presented in six parts: 1) an introduction by the dean of the University Library; 2) a review of Federal and State laws regarding equal employment opportunity, affirmative action, and the University's position by the executive assistant to the President, director, Affirmative Action Office; 3) a description of minority recruitment efforts for graduate students at the University presented by the associate dean of the Graduate School; 4) a report by an assistant librarian in the Center for AfroAmerican and African Studies on the results of a project comparing academic performance, background, attitudes, and perceptions toward faculty, staff, and students at several predominantly black and white universities; 5) a video presentation exploring the relationships in the work environment among majority and minority persons; 6) a discussion led by one of the assistant directors of the University Library.

Objectives:
To provide the library staff a better understanding of the laws regarding equal opportunity and affirmative action; to establish an understanding of the value of affirmative action in meeting the University's commitment to creating a diversified com-

munity; to clarify the library's commitment to maintaining a diversified workforce to better serve the University community; to respond to questions regarding the balancing of affirmative action with needs of the unit.

Title:
SEXUAL HARASSMENT:
THE BASICS (PART I)
and SEXUAL HARASSMENT:
THE BASICS (PART II)

Description:
A two-hour workshop for all library staff to explore the sexual and gender differences in the workplace. Participants view a short video, work on case studies about sexual harassment and gender issues, receive a brief update on the University's new sexual harassment policy, and engage in small group exercises.

Objectives:
To explore differences between males and females in communication styles and how these differences impact work relationships within the context of the University's new sexual harassment policy.

Title:
STAIRS AND STARES AWARENESS
TRAINING SEMINAR

Description:
A two-hour workshop open to all library staff and presented by the director of Services for Students with Disabilities.

Objectives:
To increase sensitivity to architectural and attitudinal barriers and staff responsiveness to persons with disabilities, especially in a library setting.

Title:
STUDENT RELATIONS WORKSHOP

Description:
A three-hour workshop teaches staff-specific skills for managing interactions with students, so that students leave feeling good about themselves and the University, and staff members feel respected and competent.

Objectives:
To enable all staff members working with students to interact effectively with the University's diverse student population; to increase the staff's ability to communicate with students of diverse backgrounds; to give the staff a clearer understanding of the broad characteristics of students and young adult developmental stages; and to help the staff differentiate between situations they can deal with and difficult situations they should refer elsewhere.

Title:
VALUING DIVERSITY

Description:
A four-hour workshop designed as an orientation for staff members newly appointed to the library. During the session, participants gain a clearer understanding of racism and personal prejudices and learn how stereotypes are formed and how they can affect interactions with others. The workshop provides opportunities to explore the issue of racism as it pertains to library staff working together and the services the library provides to the University of Michigan community.

Objectives:
To provide new staff members with a clearer understanding of the library's special role in accommodating and promoting pluralism in all of its rich forms.

Title:
VALUING DIVERSITY IN THE WORKFORCE:
THE AGING OF AMERICA

Description:
This 2.5 hour program, presented by a Social Work specialist, is designed for all library staff members and provides an opportunity to become more knowledgeable about and sensitive to this issue, specifically as it pertains to the staff working together as part of a diversified workforce and providing service to a diverse community. Topics to be discussed include stereotypes of aging; recruitment and hiring practices; legal issues; retirement laws; natural physical and mental changes associated with the aging process; and health care issues.

Objectives:
To help all library staff become aware of the many subtle ways in which age discrimination is manifested; to develop ways to ensure that the work environment supports all types of diversity.

Title:
VALUING DIVERSITY IN THE WORKPLACE:
SEXUAL ORIENTATION SESSION

Description:
A three-hour program open to all library staff and consisting of opening remarks by library administration; a review of University policies by the manager of Library Personnel; a keynote speech by the former head of the Gay Task Force of the American Library Association; a panel presentation and discussion by lesbians, gay men, and members of Parents and Friends of Lesbians and Gays (P-FLAG) from the Ann Arbor community; and a small group discussion facilitated by trained library staff members. Staff members enrolled with RSVP forms.

Objectives:
This program provides an opportunity to become more knowledgeable and sensitive to this issue of difference, specifically as it pertains to staff members working together as part

of a diversified workforce and providing service to a diverse community.

Title:
WORKING WITH STUDENTS OF COLOR

Description:
As faculty and staff of a very large educational institution, we recognize the expanding needs of our student populations. As these student populations become more diverse and sophisticated, they increase their expectations of us and expose us to a variety of communication and interpersonal styles. This two-hour workshop—presented by an organizational consultant from the University of Michigan Student Organization Development Center with extensive experience in higher education administration, counseling, advising, and student development—is designed to address these issues and is open to all managers and supervisors of student staff.

Objectives:
To allow those who work with, or expect to work with, students of color to examine how interpersonal styles can be used effectively in communicating, problem-solving, and managing conflict, and to promote a clearer understanding of how to better serve the diverse needs of students by increasing an individual's ability to understand and effectively communicate with them.

9

Supervising a Diverse Staff

Barbara MacAdam

Whether an experienced or novice manager, you probably have an image of what kind of supervisor you are, a recognition of your strengths and weaknesses, and confidence in your commitment and ability to be a good supervisor. Perhaps your library has invested much effort in identifying and recruiting underrepresented minorities, and slowly but surely, the workforce has begun to change in composition. Even though this has probably not been accomplished without considerable support and involvement of middle management staff, the hardest part is yet to come. To you, your colleagues, and your staff falls the task of working together as a team, creating a workplace environment that fosters motivation, productivity, harmony, and a sense of pride and shared goals among all your staff. As the staff comes to represent greater ethnic, racial, and multicultural diversity, this task will present an even greater challenge than in the past. The reward in meeting this challenge, however, is the opportunity to help change the institutional culture so that individuals from all racial, ethnic, and cultural backgrounds will become full and valued members of the institutional community, enriching and transforming that community in the process.

WHY SHOULD GOOD MANAGERS
DO ANYTHING DIFFERENT?

As a good supervisor, you may feel that the principles and practices that have guided you so far will be more than adequate
to handle any situation. The qualities characterizing the good
supervisor—ability to communicate, leadership, trust, honesty,
fairness, intelligence, a sense of humor—are assets in almost any
circumstance. Yet, the list must contain several other qualities:

- Sensitivity,
- Self-scrutiny,
- Flexibility,
- Willingness and ability to change,
- Acceptance of your limitations, and
- Willingness to relinquish power.

The following inventory identifies some of the attitudes
you may encounter in yourself or among your staff, in addition to some issues you may not have considered.

- Diversity means that the staff are less likely to share your background, values, and experiences. The staff will have less com-
monality in these areas among themselves than in the past.
- Former methods of communication, orientation, and training may no longer be adequate or as effective. Staff may bring
increasingly diverse language backgrounds, communication
styles, and learning modes to the workplace.
- Heightened sensitivity among all staff creates less tolerance
for criticism and unspoken fears about the changes taking
place.
- Creating a sense of shared community will be more difficult.
- The givens of the institutional culture—protocols of dress and
behavior and the unwritten rules that everybody knows—will
not necessarily be obvious to staff members of diverse backgrounds. Such implicit rules of conduct will have to be shared
more explicitly, and even more important, many of the old
assumptions will have to give way.
- You may feel less comfortable in your position and authority, less sure that you know the right thing to do.

- Matters of performance evaluation, grievances, and conflict resolution among the staff will become more complicated as awareness and sensitivity to potentially unequal barriers in the workplace increase. Recognition of the differences among individuals may create tensions between the supervisor's need to be fair and the desire to be flexible.
- You may perceive extra pressure to help staff succeed and, at times, feel burdened by the extra efforts required to foster real change in the institutional culture.
- Some staff members may feel that they are now less valued, less important than in the past.
- Increased diversity among the staff will have a concomitant effect on relations with the public.

Back to the Basics

Before focusing on the special needs of diverse staff, you must consider what elements create a positive environment for any staff member in the workplace:

1. An atmosphere of open communication.
Individuals are not penalized for identifying problems or offering alternative views. Information is shared with the staff and the supervisor listens to both the content of the staff's ideas and the underlying emotions. Ideas and individuals are treated with respect. People feel safe in expressing their opinions.

2. Trust.
Staff members feel they are trusted to make good decisions and carry out assignments well. Supervisors meddle as little as possible in day-to-day operations and are willing to give new ideas a chance. The staff members are assumed to be honest, punctual, and responsible unless there is clear evidence to the contrary. When problems arise, supervisors can be counted on to bring whatever resources possible to bear to help solve the problem and not fixate on attributing blame to someone.

3. Shared decision-making.
Supervisors make only those decisions absolutely necessary and make almost no decision without sincerely considering staff

input. Supervisors do not ask the staff to go through idle exercises in reviewing options and making recommendations if there is only one viable course of action at the outset. Supervisors are willing to accept well-reasoned decisions from experienced staff even if they are not exactly the ones the supervisor might have made.

4. High value on cooperation.
The staff feels that they are part of a collaborative team in which each individual's contribution goes to make up a greater whole. One person does not succeed at another's expense; in today's busy library, there is enough work and opportunity to go around. Staff members believe others will help them in emergencies and are motivated to return the favor when needed.

5. Self-actualization.
Staff members have as much autonomy as possible and a high degree of control over their own work. They can see the concrete results of their efforts and the stamp of their particular style or knowledge on the outcome of their work. Work is not routinely reviewed to such an extent that the individual's initial contribution is obliterated or reversed.

6. Clear-cut goals and expectations.
All staff members understand the underlying value system as well as the mission and goals of the library. Performance expectations are clear and consistent; the staff knows what is expected of them in their job and how they will be judged.

LEARNING TO CHANGE

With a productive and supportive work environment established, you should reexamine your basic attitudes and style as a manager, striving to recognize where you may have to change.

As one outcome of successfully recruiting a diverse staff, the differences in culture, ethnicity, race, and sexual orientation bring greater diversity to the workforce in terms of behavior, values, humor, dress, speech, interests, and outlook. You must be prepared then to accept and welcome many of those very changes in the context of your institutional culture, rather than trying to mold staff into an exact replica of the dominant culture that had previously prevailed. As your staff becomes more diverse in composition, so will the larger community. Be prepared to relinquish more of your authority than you have in the past. Members of your staff now may be in a much better position than you to understand the needs of your evolving user community and serve as a bridge to that community. Not only will you want to involve them to an even greater extent in decision-making, you should also willingly delegate administrative contact with the user community.

If you are, by nature and practice, a high-control person, you will need to develop a measure of flexibility and even learn to tolerate unexpected events or reactions. Your judgment may no longer adequately assess what is right or best for every situation (if, in fact, it ever did). Be prepared to listen more than you talk and observe more than you act for a while.

Finally, a diverse staff enriches the library and institutional community only if there is an opportunity for staff members to make collective and individual contributions to that community. Your staff may express interest or have involvement in a wide range of campus activities and organizations. Fostering such involvement in a realistic way gives the staff the opportunity to establish themselves as part of a supportive and meaningful community. The library only gains from such linkages.

TAKING STOCK OF THE WORKPLACE CULTURE

Each unit within a library serves as a mini-culture of the whole. It may share characteristics of the whole or differ substantively. Try to identify the characteristics of the mini-cultures inherent in your unit and library which might create barriers to a diverse staff or make staff feel marginal.

What kinds of social events do you have? If wedding or baby showers are routinely celebrated, consider the impact on gay or lesbian staff (or single staff members, for that matter) and what kind of events might foster open participation. Is Friday afternoon happy hour a standard in your unit? Many people have religious beliefs prohibiting alcohol, and if socializing in the local hangout with a pitcher of beer is a significant form of social interaction, some staff members will feel left out or take longer to develop workplace friendships.

Consider, for example, what you deem professional in terms of dress, appearance, or behavior. Multiculturalism may require you to broaden substantially your vision in this regard; at the same time, expectations of the larger culture may require you to help staff understand and work successfully in that milieu.

What holidays or events do you mark in the library, and what impact do these have on work schedules, release time, etc.? With a multicultural staff, you will encounter religious observances requiring considerably more flexibility in work schedules, awareness of dietary restrictions, and a tolerance for individual behaviors on the job. Most workplace and academic calendars are still set around the Judeo-Christian tradition, and you will find individuals who resent relinquishing the emphasis on these events. While your personnel office sets equitable practices and guidelines, it falls to you as the supervisor to make those policies work and to build understanding and good relations among your staff.

What is the underlying style of your unit? Formal or informal? Competitive or cooperative? If, for example, you have a high-stress work environment where aggressiveness and competition are rewarded, consider that people of some cultures place high value on courtesy, respect, and cooperation. In an opposite environment, people who, through their background and experiences, have learned to speak out and make people pay attention to their ideas and values may bear the unfair burden of being labeled as "aggressive," "having an attitude," "unsophisticated," or "overly emotional."

The First Step: Orientation and Training

For any level of staff, the initial orientation and training period sets the tone for their sojourn with an organization. Therefore, the basic goal of orientation and training is to successfully acclimate new staff members to the work environment and to ensure that they are able to perform their job to meet the expectations of the unit. What are some of the specific elements essential to the diverse work force?

1. An understanding of the institutional culture.

It is not fair to assume that staff members from backgrounds outside the dominant culture will automatically recognize or understand the many unwritten rules of your library and campus. While some of those rules will, and should, begin to erode over time, new staff members must comprehend the environment they are entering and must be given the opportunity and skills to work successfully in that environment. Since a new staff member will not necessarily know what questions to ask, be sure to include in orientation some general discussion of:

- How people routinely dress for work.
- What kind of dynamics the staff member will encounter in meetings or groups, and whether someone new is expected to speak up right away or to keep a low profile initially.
- The institutional hierarchy (both formal and informal) and who has unique de facto power (e.g., the unit secretary, the assistant to the library director, the individual in charge of ordering supplies).
- Unspoken expectations, such as when an invitation to serve on a committee or task force is really a request; when volunteering for a task will receive approbation; general expectations about outside professional involvement; and the importance of attending informational meetings, workshops, and social events.
- Any other useful information identified during your analysis of the library culture.

2. A carefully planned training program.

Ideally, the training plan for every new staff member should be carefully tailored to the individual coming into the position. In today's busy library, this probably remains more of an ideal than reality. As you successfully identify and recruit a diverse staff, however, training takes on even greater importance. While it is incorrect to assume that diversity and affirmative action mean that specific job knowledge and skills are automatically lacking in those joining the library under these efforts, it probably does mean that managers have broadened their awareness of what kinds of prior experience and what qualities are really essential to a particular position. Through past habit, you perhaps simply expected and hired staff with college degrees or previous library work experience into entry-level clerical positions even though the position did not require this level of education or experience. You now may have staff members who have developed their skills through experience in an office environment. Training plans for entry-level positions should then include introduction to bibliographic records, basic library operations, and academic vocabulary. In addition to content, any training program should contain the following elements:

- Clearly defined goals and timelines so that new staff understand what is expected of them. The timelines should be reasonable and flexible enough to permit adjustments as the training period progresses.
- A training atmosphere and pace that encourages communication. The supervisor or other individuals responsible for training should invite questions and make a point of asking for feedback from the new staff member. The trainer must also learn to observe non-verbal signals, since people often worry that questions and expressed confusion will be perceived badly.
- A conveyed attitude of success, so the new staff knows you have confidence in them and expect that they will succeed.
- Multiple communication and teaching modes. People learn in different ways; particularly if you have staff members for whom English is a second language, the opportunity to absorb new information should be presented in a variety of ways. Over-reliance on written manuals or on verbal communication will handicap some individuals. A combination of written documentation, one-on-one training, and audio or video materials contributes to successful job training.
- The opportunity for self-paced instruction. People absorb new information at differing rates; each individual will bring a different set of skills and abilities to the position. Building in some control for new staff in the order and pace of training and orientation conveys confidence in their ability,

reduces anxiety, and concentrates training in the areas really needed.

• Early and steady contact with other staff members and units with whom the staff member will be working. Nothing is as bewildering when you are in a new job as a sea of unknown faces and names. For staff members who worry their cultural, ethnic, or racial background may not be readily accepted in the workplace, the chance to meet and develop good working relationships with other staff members takes on added importance.

Finally, remember that your staff members and colleagues cannot help pick up on signals from you in the training and orientation process. If you act patronizing, appear uncomfortable, or convey that you lack confidence in the new staff member, people will assume that a diverse staff equates with problems. The early stages of each new staff member's tenure with the library depends heavily on your ability to make your orientation and training structure as inclusive and meaningful as possible.

COMMUNICATION: ESSENTIAL TO SUCCESS

Let us assume that you already recognize the importance of good communication between you and your staff and among staff members. Additional considerations ensure effective communication among a diversified staff. Different cultures communicate differently, both verbally and non-verbally. Forms of communication which convey courtesy, authority, and respect in one culture may be perceived as stiff and overly formal in another. By the same token, expressive hand gestures, shoulder movements, and animated facial expressions accompany standard verbal communication in many languages, but may appear excessively demonstrative or distracting to a native English speaker. Pride, assertiveness, and dignity can impart an attitude to someone who takes acceptance for granted, never having spent years proving one's worth in a skeptical and hostile society. While you may be prepared to recognize and adapt to these differences, be sensitive to the possibility that some of your staff members may not adjust as well to each others' style.

Just as people learn in varying degrees from written, verbal, and graphic information, individuals have preferred modes of communication, both in sharing information and receiving it. Some people take directives literally and follow them conscientiously, while others assume such rules are negotiable. Realistically, there are clearly times when a single form of communication will have to serve a variety of needs, but consider some of your options:

- When it is necessary to pass on documents, directives, position papers, etc. from another source, use an alternative form of communication (staff meetings, accompanying notes, e-mail messages) to highlight key items or reiterate key points.
- Sensitive or unpleasant information is generally best conveyed in person initially, even if the depth of detail requires a follow-up document. In-person communication gauges the listener's reaction and allows you to state and restate the message until it is clear; communicating directly also allows for an actual dialogue and lets you deal with questions, misconceptions, or accompanying emotions right from the beginning. Particularly with a multicultural staff, this feedback is important for you and your staff as you develop new listening and communication skills.
- Inundating staff with paper may give the illusion that communication is taking place, but usually serves to overwhelm and confuse the recipient with few compensating benefits. Be selective about the paper you pass on or route—even articles with a casual "thought you might find this interesting" note attached from the supervisor imply that the item is expected to be read. New staff members may not filter information as inherently as you expect. Going over communication mechanisms in the orientation and training program educates new staff members on what they are expected to read routinely (e.g., the library newsletter, your memos, the library's online conference, e-mail messages once a day) and what the accepted protocols of response are.
- Communication style—how people phrase things, tone of voice, body language, degree of directness or tact—probably

cause more misunderstandings and interpersonal conflict than virtually any other area in the workplace. A diverse staff may not only misinterpret your communication style (and vice versa), but also will have similar or greater difficulty with each other, as illustrated by the following checklist of common complaints about the way people communicate:

"She always has a chip on her shoulder and gets huffy if you say the least thing to her that's critical."

"He's always argumentative—a real attitude problem."

"I'm afraid to read her e-mail messages; I always feel like I'm being hit with a blunt instrument."

"He just goes on and on and on in meetings, never knowing when to shut up."

"I can never tell what she thinks. She just nods politely, smiles, and appears to agree with everything."

"Whenever there's the smallest mistake, he sends back a note that's really vicious. Who does he think he is?"

"Don't ever contradict her in meetings. She'll lose her temper and lecture us for an hour!"

"Why doesn't he ever speak up in meetings? He just sits there like a lump on a log."

The list could go on forever, but the examples all share one thing: an obvious problem in differing communication styles. Your job as a supervisor is three-fold:

1. Help your staff recognize styles of communication differing from theirs so that they can interpret other people's communication style more accurately and react with less hostility.

2. Be prepared to coach and guide a staff whose communication styles create legitimate difficulties in the workplace.

3. Carefully examine your own communication style and develop sensitivity to the perceptions that staff members of different backgrounds might have of you.

On-the-Job

With the groundwork laid for a good working relationship among staff, you must examine the possible situations and response strategies. In many areas, the needs of diverse staff members are not automatically different. There are areas, however, calling for particular sensitivity and awareness:

1. On-the-job training and staff development.

Initial training and orientation is only the first step. Staff members from multicultural backgrounds may need additional training, guidance, and development as they take on greater responsibility. The library may consciously or unconsciously tap minority staff for committee assignments and special projects to take advantage of their unique insight and commitment. In support of such efforts, you want to provide the opportunity to build the necessary skills to ensure that new expectations do not impair the staff member's ability to amass job knowledge. In the enthusiasm over successful recruitment of a diverse staff member, it is easy to lose sight of what is required to ensure ongoing adjustment and success in the position. As the supervisor, you are responsible for setting periodic review measures to assess this adjustment and work with the staff member to determine needs at each stage of the position.

2. Providing direction and feedback.

No matter how much you might hope to avoid the issue, accept the fact that direct supervision involves constructive feedback. Individuals react to praise and criticism differently; you may have to adjust your style to accommodate this. Consider a minority staff member who, based on past experiences, may feel that he is not expected to succeed or that colleagues assume he is less capable than they are. What you interpret as defensiveness the first time you offer constructive criticism may actually be a projection of these anxieties. Be sensitive to this possibility, and take extra care that feedback is neither overly fulsome in praise for routine matters nor overly critical. Both convey a lack of confidence on your part that the person will do well. Certain cultures find public praise embarrassing because it aggrandizes themselves at the expense of others. If you are sensitive to possible nuances, you will quickly observe cues that will guide you in providing feedback.

A blunter way of saying "providing direction" is "giving and taking orders" effectively. Put in this light, some problems will be hard to escape in the truly multicultural work environment.

Women supervisors, for example, may encounter unexpected barriers in directing the work of men raised in cultures in which women are not generally found in positions of authority. No matter how much you may feel that it is the staff member whose attitudes are wrong, as the supervisor, it is your responsibility to establish the basis of communication and understanding with your staff. Expect that your role as a supervisor will be more complex and demanding as the work force diversifies.

3. Keep your expectations realistic and clear.

Staff members from ethnic, racial, or cultural backgrounds less traditionally represented in the workplace are no more likely to have significant performance problems than other staff. At the same time, they are no less likely to run into problems either. Understanding, sensitivity, and flexibility are not incompatible with fairness in the workplace. One of the worst mistakes you can make is to patronize new staff by expecting less of them than you normally do of your staff. If you make this mistake, in essence, you tell new staff that you expect them to fail; you will also have fallout from other staff who clearly observe that the standards have somehow changed. One of the most important roles a supervisor can play is to create an environment for employees that helps them recognize and use their abilities to the greatest degree possible. You do your staff a great disservice if you leave them without the wherewithal to meet the organizational and larger institutional world successfully. Set clear performance expectations and provide ongoing feedback that establishes the supervisory and staff member partnership as one committed to the employee's success. If you know that a staff member has great commitment to and interest in committee services or other activities designed to contribute to diversity efforts, establish mutually agreed upon goals in this area. This will help you avoid conflict between implicit and explicit job responsibilities.

4. Evaluating performance and contribution.

Regardless of how your library's performance evaluation process operates, there are some special considerations in evaluating a diverse staff. Supervisors at any level should be sure that performance criteria are clear to the staff being evaluated and that there is no ambiguity in the expectations of the position. It is also important to be aware of the barriers the diverse staff member may encounter in the work environment. A new staff member with supervisory responsibilities, for example, may run up against an employee unfamiliar with the management and communication style engendered by a cultural background. Evaluating the performance of both employees calls for recognition and understanding in order to keep the accomplishments of both in perspective. If they successfully overcome the initial difficulties, this notable accomplishment probably offsets any decline in the unit's productivity during this period. Be prepared to recognize and reward contributions to diversity efforts, even if they contribute only indirectly to the library or library unit. If the staff takes initiative on displays or bibliographies, committee or organization service, cross-campus or community activities, make every attempt to frame these contributions in terms of the job performance. If true diversity is to characterize the library, supervisors have to find mechanisms to foster staff involvement in contributing to positive change and enrichment.

5. Fostering relations among staff members.

As a manager, you are not only responsible for the relations among staff who report directly to you, but you must also be aware of what may be involved as your staff serve in the capacity of supervisors themselves. In an ideal world, a staff who have experienced intolerance as members of a racial, ethnic, or cultural minority would be tolerant of other diverse groups who have experienced the similar barriers. Unfortunately, multiculturalism does not automatically build tolerance; people find it hard to relinquish power and commit to real understanding and inclusiveness. Conflict between individuals may increase and become more difficult to resolve. Your leadership can have a key effect. People take their cue from the respect, consideration, and understanding you display toward each of them and the commitment you demonstrate to similar relations among staff. Arranging for and encouraging the staff to attend workshops designed to enlarge their understanding in this regard is one obvious strategy, but equally effective are simple things: encouraging staff to share their experiences with each other, for example, and making it clear that you expect individuals to try to resolve their conflicts with each other before they escalate.

6. Defining "professionalism."

Without repeating the many caveats about dominant culture assumptions, it is still helpful to explore several characteristics of today's library environment and the obligations they place on staff to meet the overt or covert standards of professionalism. If you listen to staff talk about their library work environment, especially in large academic libraries, you will hear some common theses: stress, understaffing, pressure to be innovative, competition, and unrealistic expectations. There is sometimes the perception that, to succeed professionally in today's high-pressure libraries, a staff member must work to the point of extreme self-sacrifice—at the expense of health, private life, and family—to meet the library's workload as well as to make outside professional obligations. This is an unhealthy work environment for any staff member in any organization. If it exists in your library, the consequences for a diverse staff could be disastrous. Diversity may well mean that underrepresented minorities will join your staff at a later age, with significant family or personal obligations, and without the financial safety nets sometimes available to other staff. Further, many cultures place a non-negotiable priority on family, church, and social support networks. To expect the staff to sacrifice these ties is to separate them from the very communities they represent, which works against the goals of diversity. You can mitigate this environment by working with your administration to set realistic short- and long-term goals for the library in the context of institutional pressure, and by setting both a personal tone and realistic goals for the staff within your unit.

THE HARD PART: DEALING WITH PROBLEMS

Regardless of the best efforts of everyone involved, serious problems related to performance, interpersonal relations, or behavior periodically occur in any work place. An increasingly diverse staff is no talisman against these kinds of problems and, in fact, adds complexity to their resolution. We have already discussed some routine circumstances the supervisor can expect to encounter, but now need to consider the serious problems involving severe interpersonal conflict, disciplinary action, grievances, and even termination. These are the most difficult challenges for any supervisor; when it involves a staff member recruited and valued not only as an individual but also because of the experience and enrichment his or her diversity brings to the organization, the task is doubly hard. As a supervisor, you must expect to deal with your own feelings of failure, justified or not; at the same time, the staff member involved may feel, justified or not, that the negative performance or behavior assessment is based in large part on bias. In addition, other staff members will take just such an opportunity to relish the failure and attribute it to diversity efforts. Against this tension and backdrop where so many hopes and emotions prevail, it is hard to be objective and do what is fair and right. The following may be helpful in facing these situations.

1. Reducing the odds.
The single best strategy in dealing with a serious problem is to prevent it from escalating in the first place. It is impossible to overemphasize the importance of using good judgment, being aware of what is going on in your library, and being willing to address situations firmly and decisively as soon as you see them develop. At this point, you should have a good feel for where some of these pitfalls lie and how to avoid many of them. Sound training plans, establishing clear-cut job performance expectations, good communication, and regular feedback to staff have all been stressed as ways to prevent unexpected problems from occurring.

2. Sound relations with the personnel office.
As a supervisor, you should not only familiarize yourself thoroughly with any and all policies and guidelines affecting personnel matters, but you should have an established and sound working relationship with your personnel office. They will be your greatest ally in working toward successful resolution of problems and are crucial in providing direction on how to proceed when the problems cannot be resolved without of-

ficial action. The basic principle says, "When in doubt, ask." Your personnel office will appreciate such consultation and should encourage you to bring personnel problems to their attention as early in the situation as possible. This allows them to provide the most guidance to both you and the staff member, helping to ensure that things are handled in accordance with institutional policy and practice.

3. Understanding what a staff member is feeling.
Even if you feel you have been sensitive and done everything possible to communicate and work with the staff member, it is time to take another look at what the individual may now be feeling:

- "They didn't expect me to succeed."
- "All they cared about was hiring me to make things look good; they never put any effort into helping me after that."
- "People just are not used to working for (a Black woman, gay man, Hispanic man, someone in a wheelchair, etc.)."
- "People put on a show of being friendly, but I never really fit in here in the first place."
- "Just because I speak up for myself and won't be pushed around, I'm considered a 'problem'."
- "This place doesn't really want to change; all it cares about is making their statistics look good."
- "I'm always in the spotlight and more seems to be expected of me than other staff."

Obviously, feelings this profound make it difficult for the staff member to feel cooperative and willing to work within a structure that appears inherently unfair. It is also time for you to take one more look—probably with the assistance of your personnel officer—at the degree to which some of these feelings may actually represent reality in the workplace, no matter how small. Such insight can go a long way toward suggesting a new strategy for dealing with a problem that perhaps appeared unresolvable, by fostering meaningful dialogue between supervisor and staff member.

4. Facing reality.

Race, ethnicity, sexual orientation, and cultural background have absolutely no correlation with competence or incompetence, intelligence or lack thereof, interpersonal skills or their absence. As a supervisor, you cannot back away from addressing a performance problem because it will be difficult. Eventually you will lose credibility with your staff and confidence in yourself. If you are willing to commit the time and develop the necessary understanding for resolving personnel problems, you will help create a more stable and positive work environment for everyone involved.

FINAL THOUGHTS

Being a supervisor takes courage. Especially as the library and larger community becomes more diverse, you will find that you will have to take a greater leadership role in fostering the kind of cultural changes that truly transform an institution. You will make mistakes and learn from them, take risks and succeed and fail in probably equal measure, and sometimes wish that things could be easier. The commitment to diversity will take an enormous amount of time, energy and thought, competing with the many other demands made on you as a supervisor. Before you conclude that the task is so daunting, demanding skills and knowledge that you doubt you have to bring, remember one thing. If you respect each staff member as an individual and it matters to you that staff work in an environment in which they feel they truly belong, can contribute, take pride in their work, and explore their abilities and talents to the fullest extent, you will have taken the most important step toward ensuring a meaningful work experience for all staff.

10

Diversity in the Undergraduate Library

Karen Downing

For the majority of new students at the University of Michigan, their first library experience happens in the Undergraduate Library. They form lasting opinions about library use, including how comfortable they feel using the library, asking staff questions, studying in the building, and accessing information on any topic.

Because a significant portion of our primary users are continuing students, international students, students of color, first-generation college students, and student athletes, the Undergraduate Library has made a concerted effort to make these and other students feel comfortable coming into the library to study and fully use the services and resources available. It is so easy to forget the intimidation and stress experienced by new library users if we do not constantly remind ourselves that many of them come from high schools which have extremely small collections and no computerized facilities. Walking into a college or university library can be an overwhelming shock to students who have not been exposed to the number and variety of computerized and print resources many academic librarians take for granted.

In the mid-1980s, librarians at the Undergraduate Library

realized that many students of color were not fully utilizing the library's services due to barriers, such as difficult subject access to information, technological barriers, collection gaps, and inhospitable facilities. The Undergraduate Library staff took a serious look at its services and facility to see how students of color and others could be better served. To reach those students intimidated by or simply unaware of the library's vast resources, a multi-pronged approach to diversification has been taken. This approach makes staff, collections, and services intertwined and interdependent on one another.

Progress toward a multicultural organization has come through a continuous series of small steps. While change cannot happen overnight, it constantly happens in many small ways. Our goal of becoming a multicultural library still seems a long way off; yet, when we look at where we were five or six years ago, we realize we have made huge gains.

Progress at the Undergraduate Library (UGL) is unfolding in the following areas:

1. Hiring of multicultural staff.
The hiring of new staff occurred over five years. Just a few years ago, few librarians of color were on staff; today, there are two Black, one Latino, and four white librarians. The library's special minority support program, Peer Information Counseling (PIC), added 10 undergraduate students of color to the reference staff within the last few years.

2. Diversifying the collections.
A strong priority, over the last four years, has been filling in gaps in the collection in areas of multicultural collections. All selectors incorporate this priority into their areas of selection. The reference staff makes these new items more easily accessible by compiling ethnic bibliographies and new book lists and by familiarizing themselves and others with these new sources.

3. Services and programs.
The UGL staff constantly searches for new ways in which our services can be more relevant to the changing needs of undergraduate students. Services such as PIC, distributing a special minority-relevant newsletter each semester, offering special pro-

grams in the residents' halls, injecting diversity into bibliographic instruction sessions, and uniting with other units on campus recruiting and retaining students of color are some of the
ways we reach targeted students.

4. Physical facility.

A much needed building renovation during the summer of 1990
led us to consider the ways in which the physical facility in-
hibited students of color from using the library's services, finding that nothing in the building reflected the culture or contributions of people of color. Since that time, exhibit equipment has been purchased to allow the staff, in conjunction with
established campus events, to erect exhibits, display ethnic bibliographies, and hang American Library Association (ALA) and
publishers' posters. The resulting message of these efforts in-
troduces the Undergraduate Library as a place where all people
are welcomed, encouraged, and valued.

PERSONNEL

Books and buildings establish a library, but the staff makes or
breaks the success of the library's service to its campus constit-
uencies. This is particularly true for undergraduate students who
depend so heavily upon us to provide them access.

Why Have a Multicultural Staff?

In any library setting, the staff must reflect the demographics
of the university community. In the Undergraduate Library, a
multicultural staff becomes even more vital, because the size
of the research collection and the newness of the college experience easily intimidates undergraduate users. Any perceived
barriers which keep them from asking for the help they need
undermine the advances already made through service and collection enhancement. As Stoffle stated, "The needs of a multicultural, pluralistic community cannot be met by a homogenous staff."[1] Multicultural librarians, paraprofessionals, and student workers not only bring additional skills and viewpoints
to the staff but also add an extra level of comfort for many students of color.

Outreach Librarian

In recognition of the importance of actively reaching out to minority populations on campus, a new position, Coordinator of Academic Outreach Services (Outreach Librarian), has been created. Because outreach program building and network building is very time intensive, the position emphasizes these important aspects of library services of the future through several functions:

1. Role in developing the library's campus network.

A large part of the outreach librarian's responsibilities include building and maintaining the library's campus network. Producing published materials, conducting campus visitations and orientations, overseeing the development of the PIC program (and other services), and developing special partnership programs consume approximately 70 percent of the librarian's time.

2. Organizational role.

In addition to outreach responsibilities, the librarian also works at the reference desk, serves as a selector, and participates in library committee work. These responsibilities represent approximately 30 percent of the librarian's time.

The outreach librarian also has system-wide responsibilities in a multiple library campus. Many smaller divisional libraries have few staff members able to spend intensive amounts of time with large numbers of undergraduate students. The outreach librarian acts as a bridge between the Undergraduate Library and the divisional libraries. Preparing students to be more self-sufficient means making several two-way referrals between the Undergraduate Library and the divisional libraries. Should the divisional libraries wish to set up their own specific outreach programs of their own, the outreach librarian shares program development experiences and includes divisional librarians in the campus network.

COLLECTIONS

With ever larger collections and broad arrays of formats, the library easily unsettles new students and students from disadvantaged backgrounds.

Enhancing Special Collections

There is no purpose served by initiating outreach programs, inviting multicultural students to use your services, and touting the library as a welcoming environment, if there is little or nothing in the collection for students to use when they arrive.

In ever increasing numbers, schools are developing multicultural curricula. Asian American, African American, Native American, and Latino Studies departments are increasingly common on our campuses. At UM each year, we see greater numbers of students interested in exploring multicultural issues in their research assignments. Students are understandably disappointed and turned off when they come to the library only to find that materials in these areas are woefully out of date or non-existent. If we wish to entice all students to use our services, then we must have an array of materials available for them. This must become a collection development priority for all selectors.

How *All* Staff Should Work Toward a Multicultural Collection

The responsibility to build the multicultural collections lies with each librarian who is a specific subject selector. Because every selection area permits a multicultural aspect, each selector must become aware of what is available in their respective areas. We also need to broaden our views on what belongs in our collections. For example, a music area book selector, acting on the opinion that materials pertaining to rap music don't belong in an academic collection, creates a gap in the collection covering important forms of musical expression in Black and Latino communities.

Highlighting the Multicultural Collections

When a library begins purchasing items to develop its multicultural collection, the new acquisitions need publicity to alert students to this new emphasis. New selections can be highlighted in a few easy ways:

1. The age-old practice of saving book covers from new selections becomes particularly important with multicultural

selections. Exhibits displaying the book covers, both in the library and around campus, advertise the new section.

2. Putting a short bibliography of new multicultural items in the library or other campus newsletters spreads the word. Extra measures include sending the library newsletter to minority students, faculty in the cultural studies programs, and minority student services personnel.

3. Displaying the new books—ready to be charged out—prominently in the lobby of the library puts the new collection into immediate service.

SERVICES

In a multicultural undergraduate library, services reflect a variety of learning styles, cultural sensitivities, and must be dynamic and constantly updated and revised.

Peer Information Counseling

Peer Information Counseling began in 1985 as one of many steps taken to strengthen library use by students of color. Before launching the program, librarians assessed the library's environment and access to its information and spoke with student services personnel and students to gain a better understanding of the low usage. What the librarians discovered was troubling.

• There were few staff members of color to serve the increasing number of students of color.
• The building environment was inhospitable to students of color and others. Groups of students studied in their own little cliques (athletes on the second floor, fraternity and sorority members in the basement, etc.). There was nothing within the walls of the building that emphasized the welcoming environment we wished to stress for all students.
• Access to information on multicultural topics such as the African Diaspora, Asian American Internment, Native American ceremonies, and Latino health care was abysmal. With the implementation of the online catalog and many new CD-ROM products, students without computer experience were left be-

hind, and many were too intimidated to ask for help in accessing materials.

It was determined that the key to overcoming the negative findings was to have students feel more comfortable asking for assistance, and thus, the PIC program was developed. Using peers at service points in the library would allow the UGL to increase the number of staff of color, allow peers to serve as information role models, enable the UGL to reach timid students by having knowledgeable young people at the reference desk and other spots, and their presence within the library would send a clear signal to others that the UGL is a place where all people are encouraged to come. As part of the program, peer counselors would also participate in making the physical environment more hospitable by erecting exhibits with minority relevancy; they would also participate in preparing research guides to make access to the collections a bit easier.

Mechanics

When contemplating the beginning of a PIC program, consideration should be given to these points:

- Your user needs. Surveys or focus groups should ask student service personnel, minority students, and others what types of services are needed. Peer counseling? Word processing tutorials? Term paper assistance? Online catalog training?
- Discuss findings with staff. After evaluating the verbal and written data gathered, colleagues and supervisors should be asked for input. Remember, this is everyone's responsibility.
- Funding needs. A short proposal should be written outlining the types of services one intends to offer through a peer program. Whether one tries to get the program funded through the library, or through a minority student services unit, the proposal will come in handy. One should consider the specifics of how the peer counselors would work with the public each week. Other details to define include user needs, hours covered, wages to be paid, and tasks to be handled by peers.
- Finding and hiring students. Hiring hardworking students may be the easiest and most pleasurable part of running a

peer program. Many of the best students may come with few traditional library skills; however, they will have a strong service attitude and a willingness to learn. A student can be taught the Library of Congress classification system easier than the development of a helpful attitude.

- Position description. A concise and clearly articulated job announcement is necessary to recruit the best and brightest peer counselors. The document should include the responsibilities of the position, a brief description of the work environment, the pay scale, and the person to contact.

- Advertise the position. The net can be spread wide by targeting alternative advertising locations: sending the job announcement to all minority support units on campus, putting a notice in a library newsletter, mailing it to minority students, and asking students already working in the library if they know of anyone who might be interested in the position.

- Read the student publications. Campus leaders are potential peer advisors, or can direct one to others who may be interested. Student papers and newsletters can also direct one to minority-related events where there will be an opportunity to meet potential peer advisors or people who can make referrals to the program.

Services Offered by PIC

- Word processing lessons—by appointment or on a drop-in basis for one-on-one or small group tutorials;
- Term paper assistance—special one-on-one help for students researching a specific topic;
- Study tables—staffing of study table areas by PIC students builds bridges to the many campus departments which organize them;
- Reference services—basic one-on-one reference help, in conjunction with librarians or graduate students;
- Online Public Access Catalog (OPAC) training—in the library, in the residence halls and microcomputer centers;
- Research skills building—teaching information gathering in the library and residence halls;
- Tours—scheduled for special groups who need a basic introduction to the physical facility; and
- Teaching—provides assistance in the computerized classroom.

Outreach and Bibliographic Instruction

A big part of the Undergraduate Library's work is to teach information-literacy skills in conjunction with academic departments and other campus units. A huge effort has been made in the last several years to reach out to multicultural students and teach them the library skills they need to succeed at the University. Every effort has been made to make the Undergraduate Library a more inviting and vital place for all students to visit.

Bibliographic Instruction

In addition to general introductory classes being taught at the UGL, a big part of the instruction program involves reaching out to and joining with units which have large numbers of minority students.

Why integrate multiculturalism into teaching?

Many students of color regularly face barriers that other students do not.

- Some minority students come from disadvantaged neighborhood schools where computer education and school libraries were underfunded or nonexistent. They may arrive on our campuses less prepared to use huge collections and new technology.
- Because the vast majority of our staff are not minorities, students of color are often reluctant to come to the reference desk to ask questions.
- Because subject access is difficult and irregular for multicultural topics, students of color need extra assistance to find themselves represented in large and complicated collections.

Through a strong bibliographic instruction program, students who have traditionally been disenfranchised can learn the information skills they need to succeed. At the very least, they learn that there are friendly faces at the library and people who care about their success.

Examples in Classes

Things to remember when teaching multicultural students how to effectively gather and analyze information should include

- Shared communication. *How* we say things is often as important as *what* we say. Before asking students to share problems they have encountered, we should share our own—covering mistakes we made and the process of discovery. All students appreciate frankness and kindness.
- Teaching students about the bias and perspective of all materials in the library is important. For example, we should inform students about the differences between magazines such as *Mother Jones* and *The New Republic* through active learning exercises.
- Students can better understand the library's collection when they understand the historically exclusionary nature of most library materials.
- Students should know where to locate alternative sources such as the *Index to Black Periodicals* or the *Alternative Press Index* and know how they differ from mainstream indexes.
- Class examples should draw on topics of interest or current concern to some portion of minority communities on campus. Topics such as "Black Justices" or "Native American views on Columbus Day" will promote interest in the classwork.
- It is important that these students know we are interested in their concerns and their academic work. This interest can be expressed by asking them to share their topics (ahead of time when contacting the instructor or during class) and by validating their choices and assisting them with ideas on how to go about gathering information for these topics.
- Having student library workers of color co-teach facilitates participation in class as students see someone their own age serving as a role model and an information provider. They become willing to ask questions, and fear less that they will appear foolish to others. If there are minority students working in the library who might be willing to assist in the classroom, take the opportunity to familiarize them with the bibliographic instruction materials and offer them the opportunity to make a valuable contribution to the learning environment.

Special Programs and Services in Conjunction with Other Units on Campus

Although the library may be the "point of intersection"[2] on campus, it is not a place which has traditionally reached out to other campus units to form program partnerships. In the context of the multicultural university, the library will have to make new and additional efforts to plug itself into the campus network of minority student and faculty support systems to keep current with what is going on and to anticipate and respond to needed services.

Some examples of partnerships which have been formed between the Undergraduate Library and other units on our campus include:

Bridge.
Each summer approximately 60 recently graduated high school seniors who have been admitted to the University are brought to campus a half-term early. The program, sponsored by the Comprehensive Program Office, a minority support unit on campus, serves as a headstart for students thought to be at risk for retention. They take classes, attend special seminars on university life, study skills classes, and attend a special two-part library skills class where they learn to use the online catalog, learn about alternative sources, bias, and perspective, research strategies for different types of class assignments, etc. These students often go on to become campus leaders because they develop confidence and skills necessary to succeed. They are also prime candidates to fill Peer Information Counseling jobs.

MEPO.
The Minority Engineering Program Office is a unit within the University's School of Engineering. Each summer, its program brings in 7th to 12th graders and college-admitted high school seniors, and much like Bridge, it seeks to teach students what it is like to be a college student. The admitted students follow a regimen much like Bridge. These students are on campus a much shorter period of time, but are exposed to many different aspects of university life, including library sessions where they learn concepts such as online catalogs, differences be-

tween magazines and journals, fact-finding tools, library tours, etc.

*Info*Fest.*
With the Housing Division, Info*Fest is a special annual program where the Undergraduate Library "partners" with the 12 small residence hall libraries to highlight library services and collections in three of the largest residence halls. The online catalog or a CD-ROM product is set up, games such as Twister or Pictionary are played with books as prizes, refreshments are served, library literature and promotional items such as pens and pencils are prominently displayed, and the staff is on hand to answer student questions about the library. By going out into the residence halls in the evening and catching students on their way to or from dinner, one has a captive audience. Underusers and nonusers are also caught by this type of program.

Partnering with other campus units.
In order to promote library services and programs, it is necessary to enlist the assistance of all segments of the campus involved in service to minority students. On large campuses, ads in the newspapers and flyers are soon forgotten, but personal interactions with other people and units who are committed to minority student recruitment and retention is vital for passing the word about library services.

How to Build a Strong Campus Network

- Identify people and units throughout campus who have responsibilities for minority student support.
- Prioritize which units will be most important in assisting with the publicity and growth of the programs and services.
- Develop a game plan for contacting the people and units (which units will be visited, which will just receive mail items, etc.).
- Develop a short presentation of the services and programs to highlight what the library and its resources can do for them and their students. Be as creative as possible, highlighting new ideas and creating a sense of excitement and importance for the new services.

- Ask all contacts for their help in promoting the library's services and ask them to send referrals.
- Ask all contacts what services they feel are missing, what more is needed.
- Keep contacts strong by sending out regular news about the programs and services, and volunteer to assist them in the promotion of their services and programs as well.

Campuses are all arranged differently when it comes to the organization of minority student services units. Learning how one's campus organizes its support services will be imperative before embarking on strong campus partnerships. One will want to know what each unit does and how library services can complement existing academic services; the sooner this is done, the better.

Examples of Special Programs and Services

End of class "thank you" celebration.
At the end of a long semester, when students are furiously gathering information for papers and studying for final exams, the Undergraduate Library provides these students with a small break from their work. On the evening before the last week of class, we set up a refreshment area in the lobby of the library. Chips, pizza, and hors d'oeuvres are provided as a way of thanking them for their patronage of the library. This small gesture provides a lot of goodwill for minimal cost (less than $200.00). It makes the students feel good about coming to the library and provides them with an opportunity to meet staff members in a friendly environment. One should have an array of library materials on hand so that they know what types of services and publications are available to them. We send out invitations to targeted students ahead of time and make announcements on the public address system during the event.

Open house.
We host an open house at the beginning of the school year to familiarize students with the services, collections, and staff. They are provided with give-aways such as stadium cups, pens, pencils, and computer disks. The library's logo and phone num-

bers are printed on these items. Invitations are sent to targeted students, and we contact the campus network to let them know about the event.

Providing support materials.
The Undergraduate Library at the University of Michigan has published a variety of materials related to minorities for many years now. We provide the undergraduate students and campus units with

- Bibliographies on reference works, especially on African Americans, Latinos, Native Americans, and Asian Americans;
- "Did You Know" series which highlights important people of color from the four groups listed above;
- "Books By and About" bibliographies of fiction and non-fiction written by and about people of color;
- A twice yearly newsletter which highlights UGL programs, news, and services, as well as campus-wide news; and Pathfinders which highlights current multicultural topics such as Malcolm X, Columbus Day, AIDS, Martin Luther King, Jr., etc.

These publications serve many purposes including:

- Publicizing the services available at the library;
- Reminding other student service personnel and faculty about the library's services;
- Assisting students who are trying to do research on a minority-related topic;
- Operating as promotional items which can be toted to various University events; and
- Reminding students of color that they are valued within the library.

PHYSICAL FACILITY

Creating a welcoming environment in our old, and sometimes less than beautiful, buildings can be a challenge at best. There are some inexpensive ways to help renew a comfortable and welcome environment for multicultural students in existing spaces.

- Hang American Library Association and other posters which feature prominent people of color around the library. It is possible to buy frames which can attach to the wall to avoid "losing" the posters.
- Display pathfinders and other library materials which have multicultural interest in prominent areas. Clear acrylic hand-out racks in the lobby or reference area will encourage the use of these publications, as well as publicize the library's interest in these issues.
- Mount regular multicultural exhibits within the library, and promote them to minority students.

REFERENCES

1.   Carla J. Stoffle, "A New Library for the New Undergraduate," *Library Journal,* 115 (1990), p. 47.

2.   *Point of Intersection: The University Library and the Pluralistic Campus Community* (Ann Arbor: The University of Michigan Library, November 28, 1988).

11

The Diversity Librarian

Charles Ransom

"The students we are educating today will spend most of their lives in the 21st century. Theirs will be a very different world than the one we have known. . . . the structure of the American university as we see it today is a product of the 19th century . . . many of its features originated long before that in far different and distant times and places."[1]

Demographic changes will make the future American university significantly different from today's. The student body will contain more minorities. The staff and faculty will be more diverse. The library staff, collections, and programs will have to change as well to adequately reflect the new diversity.

The diversity librarian can support faculty and student research in the areas of race, gender, and ethnic studies. In collection development, the diversity librarian can serve as the specialist in race, gender, and ethnic studies. When the university sponsors campus-wide diversity programs, the diversity librarian can provide library input to those programs. Finally, the diversity librarian can design programming for the diverse library users.

This chapter bases its suggestions on methods used by the diversity librarian at the University of Michigan Graduate Library to provide:

1. Research support for faculty,
2. Research support for graduate students,
3. Assistance toward improving the library's collections in the areas of race and gender studies,
4. Support for campus-wide diversity initiatives, and
5. Programming for diverse users.

THE DIVERSITY LIBRARIAN AND FACULTY

To receive services, the faculty must first know the diversity librarian exists. Outreach, therefore, is not only an important part of the diversity librarian's job but also a foundation. First, faculty members must be targeted specifically through checking the catalog to note which faculty teach courses related to diversity. When a list is developed, an introductory letter should be sent and followed up by interviews with respondents and additional letters to non-respondents.

Outreach also includes active participation in campus groups concerned with race and gender issues. The diversity librarian should contact all minority student and faculty groups on campus to offer services. At UM, a faculty group presents faculty workshops on preparing and teaching a course in multicellular issues. UM's Diversity Librarian participates in this group, preparing bibliographies and helping with grant proposals. Outreach means being a salesperson, always looking for new ways and places to market services.

Specific Faculty Services

The diversity librarian serves as a resource person for faculty with specific information needs. When the faculty has information needs beyond a basic reading list—such as needing someone to lecture on the care of the aged in various cultures—the diversity librarian locates such a person. Should a faculty member writing grant proposals need detailed, current information and statistics relating to minorities, the diversity librarian could navigate the information maze.

To be fully utilized, the diversity librarian must keep patrons informed of new developments within the library: conducting library tours for minority faculty, holding workshops on searching the Online Public Access Catalog (OPAC) for materials on race and gender, and offering seminars focused on strategies for conducting library research on women and minorities. A seminar on bibliographic management software is also very popular.

The position also disseminates and exchanges information on ethnic, race, and gender studies. A current contents service fulfills an information need by copying the tables of contents in current ethnic, minority, and women's studies journals and forwarding them to interested faculty. Primary faculty should receive updates on library activities and recent purchases on a monthly basis.

Now that several university courses have racial, ethnic, or gender components, researchers face special obstacles in identifying and accessing needed library resources. The diversity librarian combats those difficulties with bibliographic instruction (BI) sessions to discuss the special strategies needed for library research, particularly in the areas of race and gender. The diversity librarian also assists faculty by producing comprehensive bibliographies and research guides, such as "Black Studies Resources on Microfilm at the University of Michigan."

Research consultation provides recommendations on relevant resources both within and outside of the library; mechanisms for identifying and accessing these resources; assistance in the development of computerized searching skills; and assistance with navigating informational and research-based resources and systems.[2] Research consultations offered by the diversity librarian are by demand and by appointment, and are brief as well as extended. Consultations involve locating or explaining resources, developing research strategies, compiling individualized bibliographies, and referring users to appropriate experts. For example, when the Law School asks for assistance in compiling a bibliography for a course on pluralism, consulting librarians in other areas such as sociology, economics, political science, religion, and Law Library staff worked together to satisfy the request. The research consultation resulted in a comprehensive interdisciplinary bibliography.

Services for Graduate Students

Graduate students require many of the services offered to the faculty. However, the sheer size of a campus like the University of Michigan can make graduate students difficult to identify. Therefore, outreach programs must be tailored to also locate graduate students.

Minority students often form organizations. For example, UM has a Black Graduate Student Psychology Association. Similar groups exist in most disciplines. These groups allow minority students to share research ideas and survival skills and develop study groups. By attending some of these meetings, the diversity librarian can offer services.

As Teaching Assistants (TAs) are usually graduate students, the diversity librarian can announce services to a large group by attending the TA orientation sessions. The faculty can often point out additional potential graduate researchers.

Graduate students benefit from research consultations, library seminars, and tours. All Ph.D. programs require a dissertation, and some masters' programs require a thesis. For students writing dissertations or theses that focus on race or gender, the diversity librarian can perform online searches to assist students in choosing a topic and locating sufficiently complete resources.

Services for the Campus Administration

This service, like the others, relies on aggressive outreach promotion: letters of introduction to concerned administrators and visits to targeted administrative offices on campus. At Michigan, these offices include the Affirmative Action Office, Office of Minority Affairs, Office of Minority Student Services, Financial Aid Office, and the deans of the professional schools. All of these offices have a stake in diversity activities on campus and are receptive to overtures by the diversity librarian.

The UM Minority Affairs Office sponsors a yearly Videoconference Series presented by the journal *Black Issues in Higher Education.* Before the 1990 "African-American Fraternities and Sororities" videoconference, the diversity librarian prepared a bibliography of articles on African-American fraternities and sororities. For the 1991 "Diversity in Higher Education," the bibliography prepared by the diversity librarian included selected writings by all of the videoconference speakers.

To assist administrators in becoming well-read on diversity, the diversity librarian develops an indexed database of readings related to diversity, and adds new citations each month. When the administration designs a mandatory course on racism, items in the database can survey similar course offerings at other institutions.

Another service requested at UM required compiling the profiles of 42 Michigan communities with large minority populations. When completed, these profiles included economic data, millage information, achievement scores for school children, and ethnic make-up of each school district. The UM's Diversity Librarian was also called upon to participate as a member of the Martin Luther King Diversity Day Planning Committee.

Administrators, in their attempts to develop comprehensive multiculturalism programs, routinely request bibliographic searches for books and articles on minority recruitment and retention. Additional requests seek broader and more in-depth information. The diversity librarian often becomes involved in an ongoing relationship with the administrators as they come to rely on the librarian's ability to gather resources difficult or inefficient for them to otherwise research on their own.

Other Services Provided by the Diversity Librarian

The diversity librarian also serves the library staff. For the staff's diversity training workshops, the diversity librarian produces bibliographies of related readings and compiles biographical information on and writings by proposed workshop leaders.

Responsibility for the creation of displays on library resources in race, gender, and ethnic studies often rests with diversity librarians. As resource persons, they assist other librarians in researching themes, locating materials, and mounting exhibits.

The UM Diversity Librarian also provides information to outside library professionals interested in creating similar positions and programs, as well as to others with diversity concerns.

THE DIVERSITY LIBRARIAN
AND COLLECTION DEVELOPMENT

In most areas of race and gender, the University of Michigan Library collections have traditionally been well developed, despite the limited access of women and minorities to publishing. Though that limitation creates important gaps in research, libraries cannot acquire what has not been published. It already requires much time and expertise to acquire that which is published in non-mainstream, underground, or ephemeral sources.[3]

After consulting small press directories and *The Guide to Multicultural Resources,* the diversity librarian identifies publishers, bookstores, and other distributors of materials in race and gender. Subsequent contact with these distributors gets the library placed on their permanent mailing lists. Sample titles from unfamiliar presses are requested for review. In the same process, the diversity librarian also identifies and acquires new journals in gender and ethnic studies, and purchases several important microfilm sets to round out the library's primary historic research resources.

An assessment of the collection determines its strengths and weaknesses and identifies specific issues related to each area. In some subjects, the collection is checked against published bibliographies to further identify and selectively fill gaps. Another collection assessment activity maintains a file of out-of-print materials and checks it periodically against out-of-print dealers' sales lists.

At the University of Michigan Library, each librarian functions as a selector for specific subject areas, with the diversity librarian conducting selector education: supplying information via electronic mail, involving selectors in research consultations, and referring appropriate materials. During periodic meetings of the selectors, the diversity librarian shares information on the importance of diversity selection.

SUMMARY

The Diversity Librarian's position at the University of Michigan Library is multifaceted. It has responsibilities for on-demand reference service and direct service in collection development, in addition to coordinating and facilitating reference and collection development in race and gender on a system-wide basis. Because of the position's many functions, the diversity librarian must work well with other professionals. To run a successful outreach program, the Diversity Librarian must be a creative salesperson for diversity services on campus. Being a diversity librarian is to hold a personally rewarding position that is constantly changing, always challenging.

REFERENCES

1. *The Michigan Mandate: A Strategic Linking of Academic Excellence and Social Diversity* (Ann Arbor: University of Michigan, 1989).
2. "Research Consultations," (University of Michigan Library Publications, 1989-).
3. Report of the Diversity Librarian, (University of Michigan Library, November, 1989).

12

Programs and Services in the Branch Libraries

Yolanda Jones
Darlene Nichols

Libraries of all types and sizes encounter issues of multiculturalism and diversity, often on a daily basis. This chapter will cover
a wide range of activities which libraries can employ to incorporate diversity activities into regular services. Some activities
are small and low-cost; others are large-scale and require considerable resources in staff time, money, and support. All of
them suggest directions for small- or medium-sized libraries to
pursue.

The diversity programs and services of UM's Library came
about in many different ways, using methods ranging from a
formalized and extensive planning process to serendipity. For
several years, the library profession has embraced several planning methods ranging from MBO (Management By Objectives)
and strategic planning to TQM (Total Quality Management).
Planning applies to all aspects of public services, including reference and bibliographic instruction. Many librarians who contributed their thoughts to this chapter stressed that diversity
programs and services should be developed using the same
methods applied to other programs and services, using strategic
planning methods: identifying need, setting goals and objec-

tives, assessing and assembling resources, implementing, and evaluating.

The first step, gathering facts about the constituency and determining a need for a diversity program presents a problem; often the people most in need of special assistance are those the least likely to come to the library or approach a librarian. In the case of UM's diversity programs and services, a librarian often perceives a need through interactions with students, faculty, or staff members rather than through formal methods, such as surveys. Formal information gathering mechanisms generate the most comprehensive data, but the sensitivity required to evaluate diversity services and programs calls for more intuitive or informal approaches. To reach those infrequent patrons or nonusers, the program planners must go outside the library; maybe going as far as administering surveys to campus constituents and appropriate departments, if the resources are available. A mass-mailing accompanied by an explanatory letter and followed up once or twice with requests to return the survey reaps valuable feedback from those not otherwise represented in an in-house survey or informal encounters with the librarians.

Of course, no programming should go forward without a clear set of goals and objectives. The Library issued a "Statement on Diversity and Library Services" in its report *Point of Intersection: The University Library and the Pluralistic Campus Community*.[1] The goals flow from the broader Michigan Mandate on diversity. The branch libraries' diversity programs and activities take their cues from goals set at the higher library administrative levels.

Diversity programming includes various elements: bibliographic instruction programs for specially targeted student groups; handouts about research in areas of multicultural interest; special library orientation sessions for people of color and international students; and exhibits for Martin Luther King, Jr. Day. The choice of programs largely depends upon what type of resources the library has: administrative support, facilities, staffing, and funding. Often it is difficult to provide even the basic services, much less services tailored to special needs. Small projects often consume fewer resources. Other projects can be done cooperatively or in joint ventures with other libraries or other departments in the college or university.

Special programs enhance students' educational experiences, but diversity issues can also be addressed without implementing a single new plan. Simply acknowledging the need for sensitivity to people from different ethnic or cultural backgrounds in the course of general reference services requires little or no resources. Such sensitivity applies to more than racial or ethnic minority needs; international, disabled, female, lesbian, and gay male students come under the umbrella of diversity programming. A positive contact with a reference librarian answering a question one-on-one may be worth a dozen bibliographic instruction sessions. Remaining sensitive to differences while also keeping in mind that there are also basic similarities often becomes a juggling act. A major factor in making someone feel welcome in a place is to treat that person in a welcoming and caring manner, assuring them that their interests and needs are important.

Another low-cost method of incorporating diversity into the library uses relevant examples in formal instruction. Typically, librarians use numerous examples from indexes, the catalog, research problems, and so forth, as they explain how to use library resources or how each resource fits into the research picture. Using a minority writer as the research topic in an English class, issues of ethnicity in a psychology class, the evolution of race relations in a history class, or gay rights activism in a sociology class expands the horizons of both students and librarians, making students from varied backgrounds feel that there is interest in their concerns.

TYPES OF PROGRAMS AND SERVICES
Handouts

Requiring little resources, handouts provide valuable diversity services, either as stand-alone bibliographies or as a part of a larger diversity program. Two or more libraries can cooperate on a handout. For example, UM's Art and Architecture Library and Music Library collaborated on a bibliography which listed sources of information about minority visual artists on one side and musicians of color on the other. The Art and Architecture Library also produced a two-page bibliography on "Artists Books" in support of a campus-wide symposium entitled *"Voices of*

Women of Color," as well as pathfinders and bibliographies in support of several King/Chavez/Parks visiting faculty programs. Handouts generally require little in the way of planning. An awareness of upcoming events or current areas of community or staff interest is enough. Once available, they can actively market the library by distributing them to patrons at the circulation desk, placing them in faculty mailboxes, or simply putting them in a handout rack to be picked up by browsers.

Exhibits

Like handouts, exhibits consume relatively few resources and work effectively both as stand-alone projects and as a part of a larger program. For example, the Art and Architecture Library created a slide exhibit of paintings by a Nicaraguan peasant community (Solentiname) and a poster exhibit of Caribbean-area vernacular architecture. The Physics Library, in honor of Asian American History Month, created an exhibit of Asian Nobel Prize winners. Librarians throughout the system contributed to an exhibit on Asian American contributions to American culture in honor of a local celebration of Asian American History Month. The exhibit's popularity kept it displayed in the Graduate Library for several months. In addition, the Engineering/Transportation Library worked with the Michigan Society of Women Engineers to create a display on women in engineering. The Engineering/Transportation Library viewed this as a diversity activity, since women constitute a considerable minority in the field of engineering. This same library also created a display concerning black inventors and engineers. A coincidence of publishing and exhibited schedules permitted free copies of *Campus Engineer,* focusing on women's and minority issues to be distributed with the engineering displays. Such instances of serendipity hint at what might occur with more purposeful forethought and better communication.

Planning exhibits on diversity subjects simply entails knowing in advance what types of materials are needed and saving appropriate materials routinely produced as a natural product of library over the course of the year. For example, UM's Fine Arts Library erects an annual Martin Luther King Day exhibit by saving book covers on African or African-American art subjects. A few weeks before Martin Luther King Day, they cut the book covers and mount them on colorful construction paper. Simple stencil lettering completes a vibrant exhibit. The Social Work Library culls eye-catching book jackets from new books and assembles them into themes, posting the entire book jacket display with simple banners created on a laser printer.

Even fewer resources are required in providing library exhibit space to student or other groups on campus with a multicultural orientation. For example, the Public Health Library gave library bulletin board space to the Public Health Students of African Descent, and according to one librarian, the students created one of the best displays ever seen in that library.

Tutorials and Orientations

While requiring far more labor and resources than exhibits and handouts, tutorials and orientations can in the end be far more satisfying. They tend to have a deeper impact on the students and are potentially rewarding for the library staff members as well. One instruction librarian at the Taubman Medical Library stated that their library programs create an ongoing connection between the participants and the staff. The librarian gains a sense of satisfaction in observing the students interacting comfortably with the library staff and using the library with ease.

As with the services previously discussed, these types of programs can be a one shot effort or a part of an ongoing program. Some of the most extensive diversity programs offered outside of UM's Graduate and Undergraduate Libraries have been the library orientation programs offered by the Taubman Medical Library, such as one given as a part of the Medical School's Pre-Matriculation (or Pre-Mat) Program, which comprises incoming students from underrepresented minority groups or educationally disadvantaged backgrounds. In seeking to fulfill its primary goal of giving students their best opportunity for success in medical school and ultimately in their professional careers, the summer Pre-Mat program enhances the students' academic and study skills; provides orientation to the medical school curriculum and faculty expectations; and acquaints students with available personal and academic support services.[2]

The Taubman Library's involvement with this program

shows how planning for diversity programs can be a combination of formal planning and pure chance. In July 1990, Diane Schwartz, then the head of Health Sciences Information Services at Taubman, decided she wanted to work with "at risk" undergraduate students interested in health science careers and wrote a proposal for an information management education program for underrepresented minority students. The objective was stated as follows:

> "Our efforts will focus on teaching students information seeking skills with the goal of contributing to the development of their independent, life-long learning skills to aid in the completion of their undergraduate medical education."[3]

Ms. Schwartz proposed to offer training to undergraduates in nursing as well as self-selected interested students. Later that year, another reference librarian at Taubman described the proposal to an academic counselor whom she met at a workshop. The counselor contacted the Medical School's Office of Minority Affairs and subsequent contacts with that office garnered a donation of a bibliographic database program and word processing programs to be used in the training of all medical students and in the Pre-Mat program. The library was also invited to participate in the Pre-Mat program for incoming medical students. All that evolved from a chance meeting at a workshop. Fortune favors the prepared, and it should be noted that the donation was forthcoming because a plan for a solid program, including a statement of goals and objectives, was already in place.

Thus far, the Pre-Mat program has benefitted several students, including several older students considered at risk because they have been out of school for a long period. The program is not considered remedial. The intent is to provide the students with state-of-the-art training. They learn to use a bibliographic database, word processing programs, Medline, the University's mainframe computer, and the Library's online catalog. Taubman staff, instead of doing all of the actual teaching, brought in experts from other University units to provide the most thorough training possible.

The proposal also included a library instruction component

to the orientation of incoming students at the School of Nursing. The School decided to implement only a small portion of the proposed program, but this was still a significant step. Library instruction was considered to be very important for the at risk nursing students. Nursing students are often women who come from poor educational or research backgrounds with many of them spending their first years of academic study in community colleges. Many nursing students are also older women who have long been away from an educational environment. The library orientation program taught students how to use journal indexes and abstracts; how to use the library's online catalog; and basic pointers on writing research papers. This was a one-time bibliographic instruction session rather than being part of a broader program such as the Pre-Mat program; however, programs such as both of these are expected to aid the University of Michigan in its overall goal of admitting and retaining students of diverse cultural and economic backgrounds.

Other branch libraries have also offered or planned for library instruction sessions for students from diverse backgrounds, although in a more informal manner than the Taubman Library. Librarians at the Public Health Library noticed that many patrons asked questions on minority public health concerns. In response, they planned a 90-minute bibliographic instruction session on finding information on minority-related issues in the field of public health.

The Engineering/Transportation Library

The Engineering/Transportation Library also became involved in orientation programming through its involvement with the Minority Engineering Programs Office (MEPO). MEPO's summer education program for elementary and high school students supports efforts to recruit and retain economically disadvantaged students in the field of engineering. The library in the past has helped the MEPO program by providing audiovisual support for its programs as well as basic library instruction before transferring many of the instruction activities to the Undergraduate Library which is better equipped to handle basic instruction.

Other libraries have focused on international students in their special outreach efforts. Non-native students can also be considered part of the diversity equation. In American academic libraries, the problems of providing reference services to students with different social customs, different expectations of libraries, and poor English skills are especially acute. Academic libraries face these challenges as best they can on a one-to-one basis, and a wholly satisfactory solution seems far away.

UM's Graduate Library started offering special orientation sessions for international graduate students after a staff member noted that the Undergraduate Library's open house and brief library tour were attended by many graduate students who, despite their interest, still remained unacquainted with a wider range of library facilities and services.

Open house receptions have been held for international students at the Graduate Library with staff members on hand to answer individual questions in an informal atmosphere geared toward making the students feel comfortable in approaching the librarians—a feeling hoped to endure throughout the academic year. The room was arranged to encourage mingling; chairs removed and tables shifted so the room appeared less like a classroom. One-on-one questions accommodated differing English language skills among the students. Three open houses were followed by two bibliographic instruction sessions which covered library services, basic research tips, and particularly, the use of the online catalog, concluding with a catalog exercise.

The Art and Architecture Library also offers special instruction for international students as needed. The reference librarian maintains close communications with the teaching faculty and admissions officers and, early in the semester, identifies students who are in the United States for the first time. These students are offered special library instruction because it was difficult to serve their needs in sessions for more proficient English speakers. On one occasion, when a visiting scholar arrived unexpectedly, it was the librarians at the Art and Architecture Library who referred the scholar to English-language services available locally. Sometimes this library has called upon a bilingual library staff member elsewhere in the library system to help clarify or interpret reference questions.

Even English-speaking international students may be thrown off balance by the difference between American libraries and the libraries they are used to at home. Certainly, it is easier for librarians to deal with this problem when the patron speaks English. The Art and Architecture Library's instruction for international students aids students of all language proficiencies, adjusting the pace of the instruction to match a student's level of English proficiency.

Cooperative Ventures

Many of the programs and services that have been discussed thus far have been of a cooperative nature, whether among libraries on a campus or between a library and an academic unit, such as the programs at Taubman Medical Library. This type of cooperation often creates an economy of scale. In other words, the more entities cooperating on a project, the less the effort and the resources required by each individual entity. The concept is as valid in the arena of providing public services as it is in the area of resource sharing. As one librarian put it, "It is crucial to piggyback on pre-existing efforts because it helps you to gather ideas you do not have the time to develop." Cooperation helps to implement diversity efforts in a more efficient manner. This is especially true in today's climate of chronic underfunding and understaffing.

It may seem difficult, however, to determine fruitful areas for this type of cooperation between libraries and other units on campus. The larger and more segmented an organization is, the more difficult it is to know what is happening in the other areas of the organization.

For a branch library, the easiest area to monitor is the library's affiliated academic unit. The public services librarian often cultivates contacts within the faculty to track what programs are being planned and what other activities are underway which could benefit from library support, such as when the Art and Architecture Library provided research support (by means of exhibits and handouts) for the King/Chavez/Parks visiting faculty program.

One strength of branch libraries is the collegiality atmosphere between the faculty and the librarians. Once a close relationship is established, often the faculty will volunteer information about current extracurricular speakers and programs and seek to involve the library. For example, the fine arts librarian was asked to speak at a symposium presented by the History of Art department entitled "Shaping Consciousness: Images of Blacks in Modern Western Art." The library also contributed bibliographies to accompany the symposium and a mini-course offered by the University on the subject. The social work librarian was invited to attend planning sessions for the School of Social Work's Martin Luther King Day program on multicultural social work and contributed ideas on using the library for program publicity: bookmarks about the program included a short bibliography on one side, and a bulletin board brought attention to the issues of counseling in a multicultural setting.

Librarians can also coordinate with student groups to provide diversity services, such as when the Public Health Library gave space to Public Health Students of African Descent or when the Engineering/Transportation Library worked on a display with the Society of Women Engineers. Maintaining a liaison with student groups, however, requires ongoing effort. Just as a librarian creates a good relationship with a student group, the leader graduates, and the librarian is back to square one.

Keeping an eye on what is going on in the broader university setting is also a good way of finding ideas for cooperative diversity programming. At the University of Michigan, there are major University-wide events, such as Martin Luther King Day and less regular theme events which may span several colleges. For example, the Art and Architecture Library contributed to the campus-wide, year-long program "Other Voices" (a sequel to the previously mentioned "Voices of Women of Color") by sitting in on early planning meetings and creating a brief bibliography about an African-American artist who appeared at the Art School as a part of the program, as well as an additional bibliography about artists of color.

Resources

Availability of resources such as administrative support, staff, and funding will naturally have an impact on decisions about types of programs and services to provide. New initiatives strain limited resources and basic services. They compete for funding with other important activities. They require more staff time from an already busy staff. They crowd tight spaces. Yet, providing diversity programming is indeed possible even with these limitations, when it is given priority status.

Administrative support is especially crucial in economically hard times. If library administration has made diversity a priority, it should clearly show that support for diversity programs or services even if resources are scarce. Administrators may help re-prioritize library activities and communicate programs and services occurring elsewhere on campus. When diversity becomes a central theme of library service at every level, then every library staff member will keep diversity in mind when performing their job duties. The University of Michigan Library has made much progress in this area. As one librarian put it, "I consider diversity to be an implicit part of my job description."

Outreach

Librarians can also contribute to campus diversity efforts outside of their professional roles. For example, some University of Michigan librarians participate in a mentorship program offered by the Comprehensive Studies Program (CSP), which provides academic support for entering students with relatively weak educational backgrounds. The staff participants become confidantes and resource persons for freshmen and sophomore students who choose to participate in the program. The program gives a personal touch to a large university. Universities and colleges often offer similar programs, such as tutoring or reading for the blind. The desire to help students from diverse backgrounds need not be confined to the immediate workplace.

Even when the library cannot provide its own programming, granting staff time to participate in other programs supports the campus-wide effort. It also gives the library a higher visibility and credibility by breaking into libraries' typical insularity.

It cannot be said that the range of options for diversity programming gleaned from the experiences of the librarians at the University of Michigan is an exhaustive list. Yet, the situations discussed may inspire other library staff members planning diversity services. Nothing that has been said about the process of planning is new. What is new is the recent willingness of the library community to highlight multicultural issues when engaging in planning programs and services. Ideally, years from now diversity programming will not have to be singled out for special attention, but will simply be a matter of course in all library service.

REFERENCES

1. *Point of Intersection: The University Library and the Pluralistic Campus Community* (Ann Arbor: The University of Michigan Library, November 28, 1988).
2. *Pre-matriculation Summer Program* (The University of Michigan Medical School).
3. Diane G. Schwartz, Memorandum on Information Management Education program for under-represented minority medical students (November 16, 1990).

13

Collection Development in Multicultural Studies

Joseph Robert Diaz

Few libraries focus adequate attention on collecting materials by and about our nation's minority populations. Coverage in the professional review literature of such materials, often published by small and alternative presses, is simply inadequate. Approval plans are not much better. A library relying heavily on these two methods of selection most likely has a collection of multicultural materials in need of a boost. While the ideas set forth here will probably be most useful to those working in college and university settings, materials selectors in all types of libraries ought to find this information helpful.

Multicultural collection development in the context of this chapter focuses on five U.S. minority groups: African Americans, Native Americans, Asian Americans, Latinos, and lesbians and gay men. A couple of things must be kept in mind.

1.   None of the above groups is homogenous. For example, Latinos in the United States come from many distinct cultural groups, the largest of which are Mexican Americans, Puerto Ricans, and Cuban Americans.

2. No agreement currently exists among librarians, educators or activists as to which terms one uses to describe each

group. The terms used above are the ones that this author prefers.

3. Although the collection of children's materials, foreign language materials and non-print sources is important, the resources listed in this chapter focus mainly on monographic materials for adults.

GETTING STARTED

Building and strengthening one's collection of multicultural materials begins with making a few assessments, doing some background work, and making some basic decisions.

Lobby for support from management.
Administrative support for the promotion and development of multicultural collections is crucial. In addition to controlling the collection budget, "as the policy setting body, management sets the tone and organizational culture that promotes or inhibits progress in ethnic collection development."[1] Building and enhancing multicultural collections requires commitment and work. Without managerial support, it may prove to be quite difficult, if not impossible.

Assess the demographic makeup of the campus or community.
Most registrar offices keep track of the ethnic makeup of a campus. This information reveals which areas of study and which groups need attention. Some colleges and universities may have a large population of Chinese American students, while others may have high percentages of Vietnamese American students. Even though both are considered part of the larger group known as Asian Americans, each group has its own unique needs and experiences. Therefore, the collection needs of each group will most likely not be identical.

Review current collection development policies and evaluate current holdings.
A review of the current scope, depth and breadth, and status of the collection in the area of ethnic or multicultural studies can determine how much time and energy need to be set aside for

the acquisition of multicultural materials. At this point, the collection development policy should be revised to include a statement on multicultural materials.

Decide how to fund the purchase of these materials.

In an ideal world, the selection of multicultural materials would occur in all subject areas on a regular basis and funding for these materials would come from the regular or base collection budget. Since this is not the case in most libraries today, however, extra funding may be needed initially to catch up. At the very minimum, the base materials budget should be adjusted so that multicultural materials are regularly funded in proportion to the campus or community demographics. Outside resources, such as grants, can expand or enhance a collection, but relying solely on such resources to build basic multicultural collections conveys the notion that these are special cases and extra projects outside the mainstream. Making the practice of collecting multicultural materials a part of the permanent routine requires permanent, not one-time, funding.

Assess curricular needs.

Many colleges and universities now offer courses in the areas of diversity and multiculturalism. The library needs to research the curriculum to find out what courses are being offered and by whom. Establishing contacts with faculty and others knowledgeable about ethnic studies can prove rewarding to the materials selector. A perusal of the college catalog and descriptions of various courses and departments will also reveal what a campus offers.

Although the task may seem overwhelming, work can be divided into manageable projects. For example, a library might first focus on a specific group (e.g., gay men and lesbians) and a specific type of material (e.g., fiction). After getting approval from the unit's collection development manager, the librarian in charge of the project sets a goal to collect 50 new titles in lesbian and gay fiction. Background research identifies major authors, works, and publishers. Local experts, including faculty, other librarians, and selective campus groups, are then solicited for their input and advice. After checking the library's holdings to determine what the library does or does not own, the next step identifies, evaluates, and orders the titles the library wants to acquire. The project takes less than two months to complete, after which another subject area is chosen and the above process repeated.

The following model serves as a basic framework from which to begin. Some libraries may find it useful; others, inappropriate. It does work especially well in consistently and systematically increasing the holdings in specific areas of study.

Identify an area of study to be addressed.

After assessing the campus's ethnic makeup and reviewing the status of the library's collections, it may be quite easy to identify which area of study to focus on first. However, it is prudent to extend the process to include information from other sources:

a. Talking to other librarians to ascertain specific areas they view as needing the most attention,
b. Soliciting input from faculty teaching courses in multicultural studies regarding their perceptions, and
c. Contacting campus or community organizations that represent potential target groups.

Determine the scope and depth of the project.

Setting goals affects both the way one approaches collecting materials and how much time one devotes to the project. Starting with a very specific topic simplifies the task. For example, an area such as African American studies can be made more specific by initially focusing on African American twentieth-century women novelists.

Develop guidelines for evaluating materials.

Everything associated with the focus will not be acceptable for the respective collection. Generally, selected materials should provide positive images, rather than stereotypes of ethnic minorities, and should include materials written by members of the ethnic groups in question. Few written guidelines exist in the library literature for evaluating multicultural materials for adults, but a look at the work done by the Council on Interracial Books for Children will help. In their journal, *Inter-racial Books for Children,* the Council has reviewed, critiqued, and analyzed the portrayal of ethnic groups in children's literature for over 20 years. Periodically, it publishes guidelines for evaluating materials related to a number of groups. A review of the journal, although aimed at children's and young adult materials, is encouraged.[2]

One might argue that, for scholarly or historical purposes, materials portraying racist images or promoting racist stereotypes should be kept in the collection. Libraries housing large research collections may decide to accommodate such materials; other settings may be physically unable to do so. For many years, few books portrayed non-white ethnicity in anything but a negative manner. Books by minority authors or books with positive portrayals of these groups only recently appeared. Quite probably, many collections still include more materials negatively portraying racial and ethnic stereotypes than materials portraying our nation's minorities in a positive light. Our libraries need more balance and fairness in their collections. To attain that, librarians need to educate and sensitize themselves to these aspects of selection, so that they can critically and carefully evaluate the materials they encounter.

Look for sources that list major authors and works.

Some of the types of sources one may wish to consult include:

- *Books in Print,*
- Bibliographies,
- Publishers' catalogs,
- Directories,
- Subject encyclopedias,
- Local experts (such as faculty),
- Professional review literature, and
- Other libraries' catalogs.

Keep track of those materials your library does not already own, and look for reviews of these materials.

Be creative when looking for review sources. Instead of sticking to standard trade review publications and indexes, look in audience and subject specific magazines and journals for reviews, and consult an index covering non-mainstream materials, such as Alternative Press Index. If possible, compare reviews to prevent relying solely on a single review for making a decision to accept or reject materials.

Order your materials.

Other Issues to Consider

Institutionalize the process of collecting multicultural materials.

While approaching the collection of multicultural materials on a project-by-project basis has many positive aspects, once a specific project is completed, the project's area may fall through the cracks again—additional materials not ordered, further evaluation neglected. Safeguards must be taken to ensure otherwise. For instance, small and alternative press catalogs and other non-traditional review sources must be integrated into the collection development routine. The more librarians use these tools, the more institutionalized the process of collecting in multicultural studies will become.

Create core collections.

Few resources provide a list of core multicultural materials collections. It takes creativity on the part of the selector to find core materials. Three unique titles useful for locating lists of possible core materials are

> James A. Banks, *Teaching Strategies for Ethnic Studies*, 5th ed. (Boston: Allyn and Bacon, 1991).
>
> Gary Ikihiro, ed., *Ethnic Studies: Selected Course Outlines and Reading Lists from American Colleges and Universities*, V. 1 and 2 (New York: Marcus Weiner, 1989).
>
> Majorie H. Li and Peter Li, eds., *Understanding Asian Americans: A Curriculum Resource Guide*, (New York: Neal-Schuman, 1990).

These do not deal directly with collection development, but provide useful reading lists and bibliographies that can serve as core lists. Unfortunately, the classic core collection source for college and university collections, *Books for College Libraries,* does not adequately include multi-ethnic materials.

Make multicultural materials accessible.

When a library begins to collect multicultural materials, these materials must be made accessible to the patron. Library of Congress subject headings obstruct access. LCSH terminology is often outdated, misleading, and offensive to some ethnic minorities. While no quick solutions to this problem exist, adequate cross referencing and an understanding of one's community and its preferences eases the process of providing barrier-free access. Several alternative subject thesauri and cataloging services are available throughout the country. The catalogers at the Hennepin County Library in Minnesota, for example, do an excellent job of creating timely and relevant subject headings for all kinds of topics. Their *Cataloging Bulletin* publishes the headings monthly.[3]

Librarians in the University of California system produced the *Chicano Thesaurus,* another alternative source of subject headings.[4] ASIA (Asian Shared Information Access) provides cooperative cataloging services for Asian language materials for the State of California.[5] Libraries wanting to increase access and circulation of their multicultural materials should explore these cataloging alternatives.

Fiction—Why no subject access?

Most libraries do not provide subject access to works of fiction, creating yet another barrier to making multicultural materials available to patrons. The following are a couple of alternatives that might help solve this problem.

a. Begin to include subject headings in the library's collection of fiction. Even simple identification of the nationality or ethnic background of an author is better than providing no information at all.

b. Compile research guides and reading lists of multicultural fiction for patrons.

RESOURCES FOR BUILDING
MULTICULTURAL COLLECTIONS

The following annotated list will be useful to librarians interested in finding more resources and information on the acquisition of multicultural materials. Where feasible, materials that list authors of fiction and their works are also included.

General Resources

> **Charles A. Taylor, ed.,** *Guide to Multicultural Resources* (Madison, WI: Praxis Publications, 1989).

Although it is not a conventional collection development tool, this work is useful for its numerous resource lists, including lists of ethnic publishers and other kinds of directories such as the *Black Press Periodicals Directory,* ethnic studies departments and minority colleges across the United States, periodical publications on each of the four major ethnic groups, and major ethnic collections. Also listed are a number of educational and professional organizations.

> Katherine T. A. Scarborough, ed., *Developing Collections for California's Emerging Majority: A Manual of Resources for Ethnic Collection Development* (Berkeley: Bay Area Library and Information System, 1990).

This compilation of essays and resources is one of the newest tools available to librarians interested in the development of multicultural collections. It provides coverage on a wide variety of issues related to serving ethnic minorities, including chapters on each of the following: organizing and cataloging ethnic collections, acquisitions issues, and community needs assessment. Like the *Guide to Multicultural Resources,* it contains resource lists, including names and addresses of publishers and distributors, a list of collection development consultants in the California area, bibliographies of reference and professional literature related to these issues, and sources for audio-visual and foreign language materials.

E. J. Josey and Marva L. DeLoach, eds., *Ethnic Collections in Libraries* (New York: Neal-Schuman, 1983).

A compilation of essays by various experts focuses on African Americans, Asian Americans, Native Americans, and Latinos. While it is ten years old, it is still a useful background tool. Divided into three major parts (Ethnic Collections: Challenges for Libraries; Major Collections on Ethnic Minorities; and Archives, Programming, Federal Policy, and Linkages: Sources of Strength), it covers a variety of basic issues including essays on the importance of ethnic collections in libraries and the evaluation of ethnic materials. It also contains a list of major collections throughout the country for each group mentioned.

Multicultural Review (Westport, Conn: Greenwood Press).

This new source began publishing in January 1992. It is one of the only, if not the only, collection development review journal devoted exclusively to the coverage of multicultural materials. Each issue includes news and feature articles, as well as reviews of books, serials, and multimedia materials. According to one of its promotional flyers, *Multicultural Review* "integrates work from alternative presses, mainstream publishers, academic institutions, and special organizations."

Pathways: A Minority Press Review (Chicago: Path Press).

This catalog of books represents works published by various small minority presses, including over 500 titles by and about African Americans, Latinos, Asian Americans, and Native Americans, in a broad array of subject areas, including fiction, the humanities, social sciences, and children's literature.

African Americans

Afro-American Reference: An Annotated Bibliography of Selected Resources (Westport, CT: Greenwood Press, 1985).

It lists major reference tools, including bibliographies, bibliographic guides, indexes, dictionaries, almanacs, and directories in all areas of African American studies. For the purposes of collection development, this book would probably be most useful as a guide to retrospective materials.

> Elise Burnett, ed., *Bibliography of Contemporary African American Literature, 1940-1989* (Dallas: Elise Burnett, 1990).

The bibliography contains a number of works of poetry, drama, and fiction published by African Americans since 1940. It is not exhaustive and not annotated, but useful in that it lists major and minor works.

> James E. Newby, *Black Authors: A Selected, Annotated Bibliography* (New York: Garland, 1991).

This partially annotated bibliography lists over 3,200 book-length monographs in a wide array of subject areas, including the social sciences, humanities, and literature. All works were either written, co-authored, or edited by African American writers. The span of coverage ranges from 1773-1990.

> Haki Madhubuti, ed. *Black Books Bulletin* (Chicago: Institute of Positive Education).

Since 1971, this publication, part review journal, part literary journal, has included cutting edge articles, reviews of new books, as well as essays, poetry, and short stories.

Asian Americans

> King-Kok Cheung and Stan Yogi, *Asian American Literature: An Annotated Bibliography* (New York: The Modern Language Association of America, 1988).

This comprehensive bibliography includes book length literary works as well as theses, dissertations, and journal articles. Most of the primary entries are annotated. Also included is a selective list of fiction about Asian Americans written by non-Asians. All entries are in English, although some works are English translations of works originally published in an Asian language.

Hyung-chan Kim, ed., *Asian American Studies: An Annotated Bibliography and Research Guide.* (New York: Greenwood Press, 1989).

A research guide that contains over 3,000 entries of Asian American literature in the social sciences and humanities. Included are monographs, journal articles, and dissertations. A section on bibliographies is also included.

Wei Chi Poon, *A Guide for Establishing Asian American Core Collections* (Asian American Studies Library, University of California, Berkeley, 1989).

This source provides a core, annotated list of secondary and college-level materials on five groups: Chinese Americans, Japanese Americans, Korean Americans, Filipino Americans, and Southeast Asian Americans. Included are approximately 250 monographic and serial titles in a broad range of subject areas ranging from the humanities (including works of fiction) to the social sciences. Also included are lists of publishers and distributors and subject headings used at the Asian American Studies Library at the University of California at Berkeley.

Latinos

Arte Publico Press Annual Catalog (Houston: University of Houston Press).

The catalog includes books of fiction, poetry, drama, literary criticism, and children's literature by the leading figures in Mexican American, Puerto Rican, Cuban, and U.S. Hispanic literature. Special emphasis is placed on literature by women.

David Gutierrez and Roberto G. Trujillo, eds., *The Chicano Public Catalog: A Collection Guide for Public Libraries* (Berkeley: Floricanto Press, 1987).

While intended as a core collection resource for public libraries, this useful bibliography lists a solid, basic collection in Mexican American Studies. Included in this work are materials in the social sciences, humanities, music and the arts, history, and literature. A core list of periodicals is also provided. Collection development librarians in all types of libraries should find this annotated bibliography helpful.

Hispanic Writers: A Selection of Sketches from Contemporary Authors (Detroit: Gale Research, 1991).

Over 400 authors are covered in this biographical and bibliographical resource book. In addition to providing information on Chicano, Puerto Rican, Cuban American, and other Latino writers, included are sketches of major Latin American writers. The work includes bio-bibliographical information on scholars, historians, social and political figures, as well as literary figures. This type of source does not provide critical review information, but it does contain important bibliographical information that can be used by librarians as a starting point.

Salvador Guerena, ed., *Latino Librarianship: A Handbook for Professionals* (Jefferson, N.C.: McFarland, 1990).

This book contains a number of useful essays on collection issues as they relate to Latinos. Of particular importance are the chapters on "Changing Latino Demographics and Libraries" (Eugene Estrada); "Cuban American Literature" (Danilo H. Figueredo); "Collection Development for the Spanish Speaking" (Linda Chavez); "Collection Development on the Mexican American Experience" (Robert G. Trujillo and Linda Chavez); and "Community Analysis and Needs Assessment" (Salvador Guerena).

Lesbians and Gay Men

Cal Gough and Ellen Greenblatt, *Gay and Lesbian Library Services* (Jefferson, N.C.: McFarland, 1990).

This is a comprehensive resource of information on all aspects of service to lesbian and gay populations. Collection development issues for a variety of libraries, including school, academic, and public, are covered extensively. It covers a variety of resources, including lists of core materials in a number of subjects and formats, including names and addresses of publishers and booksellers that specialize in lesbian and gay materials. Other areas include: bibliographic (subject) access, AIDS information access, reference materials, special collections, and service issues.

> Wayne R. Dynes, *Homosexuality: A Research Guide* (New York: Garland, 1987).

This comprehensive bibliography includes works published all over the world on all aspects of homosexuality. All entries are annotated. Although some in-print monographs are included, this source will be more useful for those seeking to build a retrospective collection of books and journal articles on this topic. Individual works of fiction are not included.

> *Lambda Book Report: A Contemporary Review of Gay and Lesbian Literature* (Washington, D.C.: Lambda Rising, Inc.).

This bimonthly review journal includes feature articles as well as reviews of lesbian and gay literature. This particular work fills a need not met by other review publications. Also provided are bestseller lists and new publications.

Native Americans

> Tom Colonnese and Louis Owens, *American Indian Novelists: An Annotated Critical Bibliography* (New York: Garland, 1985).

A bibliography which includes novels by Native Americans as well as criticism of those novels. Also included are other works, such as short stories and poetry. Some of the entries, although written by a Native American author, are not necessarily about the Native American experience. Brief biographical sketches are also provided.

> *Native American Authors Distribution Project* (New York: Greenfield Review Press).

This book distributor offers materials by and about Native American authors. It pulls together works offered by more than

70 different publishers. The publications range from novels and books of poetry, to children's literature, journals and newspapers, how-to books and history, all by authors of Native American ancestry.

> Barry T. Klein, ed., *Reference Encyclopedia of the American Indian,* 5th ed. (West Nyack, N.Y.: Todd Publications, 1990).

Divided into four main sections, this work includes an unannotated bibliography, organized by title and subject, of approximately 4,000 titles of in-print books about Native Americans. It also contains lists of Native American periodicals and publishers.

REFERENCES

1. Albert J. Milo and Luis Herrera, "Managing Administrative Change for Ethnic Collection Development," *Developing Library Collections for California's Emerging Majority: A Manual of Resources for Ethnic Collection Development* (Berkeley: University of California, 1990), pp. 20-21.
2. *Interracial Books for Children Bulletin* (New York: Council on Interracial Books for Children).
3. *Cataloging Bulletin* (Hennepin County Library). This source is published six times a year; it lists all the new subject headings created by the staff at the Hennepin County Library in a given two-month period. A great deal of attention is paid to creating subject headings which are timely, culturally sensitive, and relevant.
4. *Chicano Thesaurus for Indexing Chicano Materials* (Committee for the Development of Subject Access to Chicano Literature, University of California, Berkeley). This work began in 1977 to more accurately reflect the natural language of Chicanos, which is a mixture of English, Spanish, and Calo. It is now available as part of the *Chicano Periodicals Index* (both in paper and CD-ROM).
5. *ASIA* (Asian Shared Information Access) The following two articles describe in detail the work ASIA does:
   A. Russell G. Fischer, "Project ASIA: California Public Libraries Serving the Asian Community," 111 *Library Journal* (1986), 62-64.
   B. Kate Seifert, "Bringing Generations of New Americans to Our Public Libraries," 27 *California State Library Foundation Bulletin,* (1989), p. 4-5.

14

Exhibits

Janis Apted Giannini

Early in the implementation of its diversity program, the University of Michigan Library decided that exhibits could provide a visually appealing, non-threatening way to present new information concerning diversity-related topics. Imaginative, colorful displays offer visual evidence that the library welcomes all cultures and philosophies.

Since UM's program began, the staff in various University Library facilities has created many different displays. Some celebrated minority culture: "The Rulers of Africa" exhibit in the Serials Division; "Paintings and Sculptures by African American Artists" in the Art and Architecture Library; "People of Color in the History of Art" in the Fine Arts Library; and "Diversity through Literature" in the Graduate Library. Others celebrated well-known Blacks like the Natural Science Library's display on Martin Luther King. The Rare Books and Special Collections Library mounted two exhibits—"African Americans in American Culture" and "The Civil Rights Movement"—using original copies of rare materials housed in that library.

Some libraries gave attention to minority professionals: Taubman Medical Library mounted exhibits on "The History of African American Women" and on the research interests of minority faculty at the University of Michigan Medical School and Hospital; the Engineering Library, in ongoing cooperation with the Minority Engineering Program Office, focused on minority engineers; and the Music Library featured two displays devoted to African American musicians.

Small groups of staff design and mount many of these exhibits. A subcommittee of the Library's Diversity Committee regularly places seven to eight exhibits a year in the Graduate Library while volunteers continue to create exhibits in the divisional libraries.

In the midst of chaotic work days, exhibits may seem a luxury.

With limited staff and resources, it is easy to eliminate designing exhibits, postponing the challenge of creating bold and exciting displays to the future when there is enough time, staff, money, and computers for graphics. Even with basic components available, difficulties may arise in developing ideas and locating reference resources. What holidays, festivals, and special events can be used as themes? What materials are available? What constitutes a fair, impartial, and informative presentation of a diversity-related issue?

The experience of the University of Michigan Library indicates that exhibits do not have to be unnecessarily difficult or time-consuming to plan and mount. With very few resources and some creative thinking, good displays can delight students, faculty, and visitors, become favorite places to stop and take in something new and interesting.

SIX REASONS FOR DIVERSITY-RELATED EXHIBITS

1. A strong exhibits program makes a powerful, visual statement about the content and scope of the library's collections.

It is not enough to purchase and house extensive collections if few people know they exist. As with any product of service, the library's collection needs promotion. Librarians have been quick to adopt sophisticated marketing techniques, including the art of book displays. These exhibits stimulate the interest of passersby, further benefitting the overall public relations effort.

2. Libraries have to compete for the attention of readers.
With an increasingly wide range of leisure time activities (cable television, videos, CDs, personal computers, etc.) and locations (shopping malls, theaters, entertainment center-equipped homes, etc.), libraries must create an enticing environment to attract both the busy occasional patron and the more reluctant library user. Colorful, creative displays generate a more friendly, welcoming place where visitors will want to linger.

3. Exhibits attract new readers by promoting information of interest and relevance to a range of ethnic and racial backgrounds.
Special efforts must be made to attract people coming from areas of the world where libraries are not readily available. Exhibits can draw minority users with culturally familiar materials and information that speaks to their needs. The library's collections and its public relations effort, including exhibits, should reflect the growing diversity of its community. In promoting its products and services, the library builds support within its community by demonstrating its desire to respond to the needs of a diverse constituency.

4. For the library user with habitual reading patterns, exhibits open doors to new areas of interest, providing glimpses of different cultures, beliefs, and points of view.
As society becomes more multicultural, the library's collections help readers understand more about the changing fabric of their local and global community. All readers, from those with defined reading habits to those with none, need to be encouraged to explore new areas of interest.

5. Librarians have access to collections of great depth and scope.
By pulling books from the collection into displays with diversity-related themes, librarians offer readers an opportunity to experience the multicultural character of their own communities. An exhibit for Black History Month, for example, can bring together diaries, histories, literature, maps, and non-print

materials to provide a unique perspective on some aspect of African-American history.

6. Diversity-related exhibit themes also sensitize the library staff to multicultural issues.

In working through a theme, the staff must select appropriate materials and cull interesting facts. Developing exhibits with a culturally diverse group enriches the experience as thoughts, values, and beliefs are shared and individual cultural blind spots are revealed. Mounting exhibits meaningful and interesting to the library's target audience requires an understanding of the potential user's concerns. Ideally, the staff responsible for diversity-related exhibits will educate themselves on the cultural structure of the population they serve.

Librarians should aim to have more and better informed library users in our communities, no matter what their ethnic and racial backgrounds. Exhibits function as a part of public relations, and as Mark Schaeffer writes in the preface to his *Library Displays Handbook,*

> [A]n effective public relations program is vital to the success of any library—public, school, academic, or special. People today are busier than they've ever been. They are faced with an overwhelming array of activities, at home, at school, and at the office, all of which compete for limited time and money. Without a dynamic, ongoing, effectively designed public relations program to promote our services and products, libraries will simply get lost in the shuffle. Worse yet, if people don't know why we're important, the library will also be forgotten when it comes time to make funding decisions."[1]

Our public relations effort must reach all segments of our potential user population: Asians, Blacks, Hispanics, Native Americans, and other ethnic and racial groups as well as the Anglo-American library user.

Creating Effective Exhibits

Without training in exhibit design, the thought of creating effective displays can cause designer block. Tackling multicultural issues may add to the feeling of paralysis. No matter what kind of space is available for displays—small bulletin boards, standing panels, wall or window cases, or professional exhibit cases—certain basic design concepts help ensure an effective, aesthetic result. Common sense guides the five major design principles (balance, emphasis, simplicity, variety, and unity). By learning the basics of design principles and elements (line, shape, space, color, and texture), one has a greater chance of creating successful exhibits.

Balance

A pleasing distribution of display elements produces balance in a design. In other words, the design feels right, with no part of the whole looking askew or too heavy. Designers refer to balance as visual weight. Where balance is achieved, the display emits a harmonious feel. Where balance is not achieved, the display items appear to be strewn through the space in no recognizable pattern. The eye finds no place to settle.

Symmetry achieves one form of balance. Easy to accomplish, one half of a design simply mirrors the other half. Because symmetry produces such an obvious balance, it is often over-used, resulting in boring displays that somehow always look alike. Visual weight is the key to effective asymmetrical designs: distributing weightier objects (those that are bold, big or bright) in such a way that they are balanced by the less weighty items in the design. When laying out the exhibit pieces before mounting them, the issue of weight becomes immediately apparent. Experimenting with different layouts will find the most pleasing balance for the specific materials.

Emphasis

Nothing creates more frustration than an unfocused display of hodge-podge. Every design should emphasize some element. Emphasis can be achieved through heightening the visual weight of an object by making it brighter, bigger or bolder; mounting the object on special paper to highlight it; placing the item in a prominent spot in the display; and for text, using a different typeface such as italic or bold.

Simplicity

In most cases concerning design, less is more. A display should accomplish its purpose as simply as possible, using only what is necessary. This does not mean visual appeal must be sacrificed to simplicity as that would defeat the purpose of an exhibit. Decisions about what to include or what to eliminate from a design involve careful judgment. The decisions themselves are often subtle in nature.

Variety

The principle of variety flatly contradicts the principle of simplicity. It states that every design should include the "greatest possible variety of shapes, sizes, type styles, colors, textures, and so on."[2] The abundance of design options adds to the fun of creating a stunning effect. The principles of design are guidelines, not rigid rules. Only our intuition can determine how to achieve simplicity without foregoing the delights of variety. As in any learning process, mistakes provide opportunities and experience to know what works and what does not.

Unity

If the design parts create a whole, unity or harmony has been achieved. Unity is the supreme principle, embodying every other principle and convention of good design. "If you create a design that is visually balanced, if you emphasize the important elements, if you choose colors that look good together, if your type styles and illustrations are appropriate to your theme, and if you strike a reasonable compromise between simplicity and variety, then the result is likely to be a unified design."[3] This may sound like an impossible goal but through working with the design of displays, applying these principles becomes second nature. The guidelines of balance, emphasis, simplicity, variety, and unity allow us to use the basic elements of design effectively—line, space, shape, color and texture.

Line

Lines give order to the design. They draw the observer's eye to a certain area of the design, the focal point of interest. Lines bring together related things and separate the unrelated.

Lines can be visible or invisible. Visible lines, whether thick, thin, straight, curved, jagged, continuous, or broken, communicate moods and feelings. Different types of lines play different roles. For instance,

> stability = straight lines
> unpredictability = diagonal lines
> fun = curved or wavy lines
> excitement = jagged lines

Lines serve as borders to enclose important information, as dividers to separate information, or as decorative devices such as borders. Invisible lines also bring order. Objects placed at random in a display case are rarely as effective as those aligned. Invisible lines separate objects and define the pattern in the design.

Shape

Shape gives a design substance and visual impact. Neglecting shape begets the tired look of one thing lined up with another in block-like formation.[4]

Space

The appropriate use of space adds a sense of freedom. Less is more remains a good rule of thumb. Plenty of open space makes the display more inviting and visually appealing, whereas crowded exhibits defeat the viewer from the outset. A jam-packed display case requires too much time and effort from the passerby.

Color

Colors bring emotion to a display. In multicultural exhibits, using the colors favored by different cultures establishes the tone and mood. The more colorful and bold the exhibit, the more attention it will attract. For instance, a display in the vivid colors of Mexico—hot pink, bright yellow, vibrant red, and brilliant turquoise—evokes a lively, Latin mood for Hispanic Heritage Month.

Department store windows contain wonderful color combination ideas to imitate. Successful window designers have an often breathtaking flair for color. A clipping file created from decorating and fashion magazines helps keep imaginative color effects readily at hand.

Texture

While not usually meant to be touched, library exhibits should be so rich in texture that the viewer instinctively wants to reach out for them. Multicultural materials that add texture include fabrics from various cultures; Native American pipes, feathers, and dream catchers; Chinese bowls and objects d'art; relief maps made of foam core board; and myriad other things. Local stores may be willing to loan items, and the staff can bring things from home.

User response to exhibits tells how successfully the principles and elements of design have been applied. If the results are less than desired, comfort can be found in knowing a mistake made is a lesson learned.

THE ADVANTAGE OF GROUP CREATIVITY

The University of Michigan Library's Diversity Exhibits Committee selects themes and designs and mounts the exhibits. A committee works well for this kind of task for a number of reasons:

1. The group synergy produces a wide range of creative ideas and approaches, resulting in more exciting displays.

2. A multicultural committee allows staff to learn from each other as they work on topics new to some of them.

3. Different cultural perspectives ensure that multicultural themes are treated with sensitivity.

4. Divided labor lessens the work load and gives everyone some responsibility: research, gathering appropriate supplies, lettering and artwork, layout, and then, mounting the display pieces.

5. Exhibit expertise is spread throughout the library; more people can help with almost any aspect of exhibits.

SELECTING THEMES

Selected themes should interest the library's community. A good grasp of local demographics is essential. A display celebrating the Vietnamese New Year, when no Vietnamese reside in the area, might not be the best use of exhibit space.

Having chosen an appropriate theme, the topic must then receive impartial and sensitive treatment. Library exhibits are not meant to be controversial. Stirring up controversy can create community ill-will toward the library—a public relations fiasco. If the theme is a multicultural issue, information should represent the varying points of view. An exhibits committee that is multicultural in its own make-up can monitor theme presentation to prevent exhibits from becoming individual soap boxes or misguided efforts to persuade library users. Cultural insensitivity undermines the purpose of the exhibit.

A vast array of festivals, holidays, and special or historical events make interesting exhibit themes. The specific date of some events changes annually according to the calendar. Consulates, embassies, religious associations, and ethnic social clubs can supply dates and celebrational information for a specific culture's special events. They may also have posters and other materials appropriate for the exhibit. The University of Michigan checks the Office of Minority Affairs and the Minority Student Services Office to find out about events, establish dates, and collect or borrow exhibit items.

Exhibits should remain fresh and timely for a month. Given the work involved in planning and mounting displays, one will want to choose themes carefully and plan a yearly calendar of exhibit topics. The following list is presented as an example. It is not definite nor complete.

JANUARY

Independence Day: *Haiti* (January 1, 1804)
                      Sudan (January 1, 1956)
                      Burma (January 4, 1948)
                      India (January 26, 1929)

New Year's Day: Celebrated by many countries: *Korea, Taiwan, Japan, Thailand, etc.* (January 1)

Chinese New Year: *China*'s celebration (late January or early February)

Kite Festival: *India* hosts a kite-flying festival as a traditional way of celebrating the first day of spring (January 14)

Adults' Day: *Japan*'s national holiday honoring young people who have achieved adulthood during the past year (January 15)

M. L. King Day: *U.S.* honors Martin Luther King, Jr.'s contributions and nonviolent approach to civil rights issues (January 15)

Constitution Day: Philippines remembers the day the amended constitution was ratified in 1935 (January 17)

Republic Day: *India* celebrates their 1929 independence (January 26)

FEBRUARY

Independence Day: *Sri Lanka* (February 4, 1948)
                      Grenada (February 7, 1974)
                      St. Lucia (February 18, 1965)
                      Dominican Republic (February 27, 1844)

Black History: *African American* remembrance and recognition of their contributions and achievements (month of February)

Powamu Festival:	*Native American* celebration of the creation of men, women, and the earth itself (January 3)
National Freedom:	*U.S.* outlawed slavery on this date in 1865 (February)
Elizabeth Blackwell Birthday:	*Women* now follow in the footsteps of Blackwell—the first female physician in this country (February 3, 1821)
Setsubun:	*Japan* celebrates the last day of winter, according to the lunar calendar, to drive out evil spirits and welcome good ones in. Also known as the "Beam Throwing Festival" (date varies annually)
Constitution Day:	*Mexico*'s present constitution was adopted in 1917 (February 5)
Japan Empire Day:	*Japan* marks its 660 B.C. founding by emperor Jimmu Tenno (February 11)
NAACP Founded:	*U.S.* In 1909, the National Association for the Advancement of Colored People was established to work toward eliminating discrimination against people of color (February 12)
Race Relations Day:	*U.S.* designated this day for recognizing the importance of interracial relations (February 14)
Susan B. Anthony:	*Women*'s rights activist Anthony was born in 1820 (February 15)
Tet:	*Vietnam* celebrates the beginning of spring and the new year (approximately February 15-17)
Brotherhood, Sisterhood Week:	*U.S.* recognizes and honors the equality among all racial, ethnic, and religious groups (third week of February)
Wounded Knee:	*Native American* remembrance of the 1873 taking of the town of Wounded Knee, South Dakota by supporters of the American Indian Movement (February 28)

MARCH

Independence Day:	*Korea* (March 1, 1919) *Ghana* (March 6, 1957) *Mauritius* (March 12, 1968) *Tunisia* (March 20, 1956) *Bangladesh* (March 26, 1971)

Lantern Festival:	*China* concludes the Chinese New Year with a traditional lantern procession (date varies annually)
Hina Matsuri:	*Japan* honors girls by displaying dolls in Japanese homes (March 3)
Black Press Day:	*African American* newspaper called *Freedom's Journal* was first published in New York in 1827 (February 16)
Ramadan:	*Islamic* period of fasting falls in the ninth month of the Islamic calendar and lasts for thirty days (date varies)
Emancipation:	*Puerto Rico* abolished slavery this date in 1873 (March 22)
Martyr's Day:	*Taiwan* honors its martyrs (March 29)
Youth Day:	*China* honors its young adults (March 29)

APRIL

Independence Day:	*Senegal* (April 4, 1960) *Zimbabwe* (April 18, 1980) *Togo* (April 27, 1960)
Older Americans' Month:	*U.S.* can gain awareness of the active lifestyles of older Americans with assistance from the American Association for Retired Persons exhibit materials (entire month)
Civil Rights Act:	*U.S.* President Lyndon Johnson signed the law in 1968, protecting individuals from discrimination in housing (April 11)
Song Kran Festival:	*Singapore and Thailand* hold a New Year's festival (mid-April)
Idul-Fitr:	*Islamic* festival concluding the end of the month of Ramadan fasting (date varies according to Islamic calendar)
Kartini Day:	*Indonesia* celebrates Raden Adjeng Kartini, the leader of the emancipation of women (April 21)

Buddha:	*Buddhists* honor the birthday of Buddha circa 560 B.C.; primarily for India, China, Japan, Korea, Vietnam, and Tibet (approximately April 8)
Pan-American Day:	*The Americas* recognize Latin and North American cultures (April 14)

MAY

Independence Day:	*Paraguay* (May 14, 1811) *Argentina* (May 25, 1810)
Asian/Pacific Heritage Week:	(first full week in May)
Cinco de Mayo:	*Mexico*'s national holiday celebrating the 1862 battle when Mexican defeated French invaders (May 5)
Kodomo-no-hi and Children's Day:	*Japan and Korea* honor children (May 5)
American Indian Day:	*American Indians,* since May 13, 1916, have been honored on either the second Saturday in May or the fourth Friday in September.
Malcolm X:	*African American* civil rights activist and black nationalist's birth in 1925 is commemorated (May 19)
African Freedom Day:	*Zambia, Chad, Mauritania, and other African states* have dedicated this day to labor, freedom, and national productivity, since the 1963 formation of the Organization of African Unity (May 25)
Indian Removal Act:	*Native American* remembrance of the day President Andrew Jackson signed legislation leading to the tragic event now known as the "Trail of Tears" in which thousands of American Indians died in 1830 in being forced to leave their homes in the east and walk to the western lands assigned to them by the government (May 28)

JUNE

Independence Day:	*Philippines* (June 12, 1898) *Zaire* (June 23, 1960) *Madagascar* (June 26, 1960)
Black Music Month:	*Black* musicians' contributions to the world of music honored (month-long)
King Kamehameha I:	*Hawaii* celebrates the birthday of King Kamehameha (1737-1819) who increased foreign trade while driving out the island's invaders (June 11)
Death of Mohammed:	*Islamic* mourning of the 632 A.D. death of Mohammed (June 8)
Juneteenth:	*African American* remembrance of the day slaves were freed in Texas in 1865 (June 19)
Custer's Last Stand:	*Native Americans* mark the 1876 defeat of Custer at the Battle of Little Big Horn, a major event during the Indian wars and another tragedy of the westward expansion in the U.S. (June 25)
Helen Keller:	*Physical impaired* Keller's 1880 birthday celebrates her incredible accomplishments as an author and lecturer despite being born physically impaired, making her an American legend (June 27)

JULY

Independence Day:	*Burundi* (July 1, 1874) *Rwanda* (July 1, 1962) *Cape Verde* (July 5, 1975) *Venezuela* (July 5, 1811) *Malawi* (July 6, 1966) *Bahamas* (July 10, 1973) *Colombia* (July 20, 1819) *Liberia* (July 26, 1847) *Peru* (June 28, 1821)
Civil Rights Act:	*U.S.* President Lyndon B. Johnson signed this act in 1964, forbidding racial discrimination in employment and in public places (July 2)

Friendship Day:	*Philippine American* celebration (July 4)
Muharram:	*Islamic* New Year (date varies annually)
O-Bon:	*Japan's* Festival of Lanterns held in memory of the dead (mid-July date varies annually)
Ratha-yatra:	*Hindu* New Year (date varies)
Nelson Mandela:	*South African* civil rights leader's 1918 birth-date celebrated (July 17)
Constitution Day:	*Puerto Rico* celebrates the 1952 ratification of its Constitution (July 25)

AUGUST

Independence Day:	*Malaysia* (August 1, 1957) *Bolivia* (August 6, 1825) *Jamaica* (August 6, 1962) *Ivory Coast* (August 7, 1960) *Singapore* (August 9, 1965) *Ecuador* (August 10, 1809) *Chad* (August 11, 1960) *India* (August 15, 1947) *Indonesia* (August 17, 1945) *Uruguay* (August 25, 1828) *Trinidad and Togbago* (August 31, 1962)
Peace Festival:	*Japan* remembers the victims who were killed when the first atomic bomb was dropped on Hiroshima in 1945 (August 6)
Youth Day:	*Zambia* honors young people (August 6)
Moment of Silence:	*Japan's* memorial day noting the second atomic bomb, dropped on Nagasaki in 1945 (August 9)
Alex Haley:	*African American* author of *Roots,* born in 1921 (August 11)
Pueblo Revolt:	*Native Americans,* Pueblo Indians and their Apache allies, drove the Spaniards out of New Mexico in 1680 (month of August)
Women's Equality Day:	*Women's* rights movement recognized (August 26)

Geraldine Ferraro: First *woman* to run for U.S. Vice President, born in 1935 (August 26)

SEPTEMBER

Independence Day: *Vietnam* (September 2, 1945)
Swaziland (September 6, 1968)
Brazil (September 7, 1822)
Guinea-Bissau (September 10, 1974)
Mexico (September 15-16)
Costa Rica, El Salvador, Guatemala, Honduras, and Nicaragua (September 15, 1821)
Papua New Guinea (September 18, 1818)
Belize (September 21, 1981)
Botswana (September 30, 1966)

National Revolution Day: *Ethiopia* (September 12, 1974)

National Day: *St. Kitts and Nevis* (September 19, 1983)

National Hispanic Heritage Month: *Hispanic* (September 15-October 15)

Moon Festival: *China*'s harvest festival, celebrated with special "moon" cakes, to give thanks to ancestors (September 22)

Chusok: *Korea*'s harvest moon festival (September 22)

American Indian Day: *Native Americans* honored (fourth Friday in September or second Saturday in May)

Confucius: *Chinese* philosopher's 551 B.C. birthday celebrated (date varies according to Chinese calendar)

OCTOBER

Independence Day: *Nigeria* (October 1, 1960)
Guinea (October 2, 1958)
Lesotho (October 4, 1966)
Uganda (October 9, 1966)
Fiji (October 10, 1970)
Equatorial Guinea (October 12, 1968)
Zambia (October 24, 1964)

National Day:	*China* (October 1, 1949) *Somalia* (October 21, 1969)
Alphabet Day:	*Korea*'s King Sejong of the Yi Dynasty adopted the 24-letter alphabet on this day in 1446 (October 9)
Dia de la Raza:	*Hispanic* countries celebrate the common heritage of Spanish and Indian peoples (October 12)
Black Poetry Day:	*African American* poets receive recognition on the day of the 1711 birth of Jupiter Hammon, the first published Black American poet (October 17)

NOVEMBER

Independence Day:	*Panama* (November 3, 1903) *Suriname* (November 25, 1975) *Mauritania* (November 28, 1960) *Barbados* (November 30, 1966)
National Day:	*Angola* (November 11, 1975) *Benin* (November 30, 1966)
Diwali:	*India* lights lamps and places them in the windows of Indian homes in the hopes that they will bring prosperity to the occupants (November 5)
Marie Curie:	*Woman* chemist and physicist's 1867 birthday honors her as one of the premier women of science and Nobel prize winner (November 7)
Children's Day:	*India* honors children (November 14)
Shichi-Go-San:	*Japan* honors children aged 7, 5 and 3 (November 15)
Discovery Day:	*Puerto Rico* celebrates its 1493 discovery (November 19)
Sojourner Truth Day:	*Abolitionist and women's rights* leader's 1883 day of death commemorates her lifelong struggle against slavery and for women (November 26)

DECEMBER

National Day: *Central African Republic* (December 1, 1965)
       Laos (December 2, 1954)
       Thailand (December 5, 1927)
       Bhutan (December 17, 1949)

Republic Day: *Niger* (December 18, 1960)

Day of Quito: *Ecuador* marks the 1534 founding of its capital (December 6)

Jamhuri Day: *Kenya*'s National Day commemorates the 1963 beginning of its republic (December 12)

Kwanzaa: *African* week-long series of activities recognizing traditional harvest festivals, acknowledging the unity of the family, and concluding with a karamu (feast) at the end of the week's festivities. (December 26-31)

DESIGNING AND PRODUCING EXHIBIT PIECES

1. Determine the size and amount of display space available.

Will the display be on a bulletin board, in wall cases or exhibit cases, on a table or a shelf? What are the peculiarities of the space? For example, each wall case in UM's Harlan Hatcher Graduate Library has three wood-framed glass doors, cutting the space into three tall, narrow, and difficult spaces. With no lighting fixtures installed inside, the cases are very dark. We compensate for the lack of light by using strong, bright colors and neutral, light backgrounds.

2. Use the elements and principles of design to draw a preliminary sketch of the design.

Cut-out shapes representing the display materials can be shifted around to create different arrangements for the sketch or materials can be laid out on the floor to determine the best design.

3. Select items from the collection to include and decide on other supplemental material.

Consider what tone to create with colors, texture, and so on. Decide what text will identify and unite the materials, and create a short, catchy title.

4. Assemble the tools and supplies needed:

Fabric, construction paper, scissors and cutting knives, lettering kits, poster board, glue, staples and staple gun, stick pins, and tacks.

5. Prepare the heading, labels, and graphic images.

These can be done by hand or with a computer graphics package. Plans may change at this point as new ideas arise. The creative process does not stop at any one point. Even while mounting the exhibit, changes may occur.

6. Plan to store the old exhibit materials.

A resource file of ready materials saves future time and money. Virtually every part of an exhibit can be reused or adapted for another display. Polaroid photos of the exhibit make a record of what each exhibit contained. Unused exhibit items should also be saved in the resource file.

TIME AND COST FACTORS

Starting from scratch in both materials and experience makes the first exhibit the most difficult and time consuming. With experience in locating and buying supplies, producing labels and text, and mounting the final display, exhibits become easier and faster to accomplish.

- Select theme, decide on the message of the exhibit, make a list of materials to be featured, discuss how excitement or drama will be created, make committee assignments (if needed).

1-2 hours

- Select book jackets or books and other materials such as art objects, write text for labels, decide on title and discuss any artwork that needs to be done.

2-3 hours

• Prepare headline (title), labels, text, and produce artwork.

3-5 hours

• Mount exhibit.   1 hour

More elaborate exhibits take longer but allowing for 10 hours of work is an appropriate guideline. An experienced group of individuals sharing the work can produce exhibits in less time.

Costs are minimal. An exhibit can be done for $10 to $15 using simple supplies like construction paper, glue, an X-acto knife, and stick pins. A good lettering kit costs about $85 and should be an essential tool even in conjunction with computer graphics programs. Posters and other visual material ordered from catalogs generally cost $20 to $30. Special artwork produced by the student graphics shop adds a little extra expense.

Involved exhibit work makes use of an endless number of supplies: acrylic paint, calligraphy tools, clip art, cutting mats, fabric paint, layout grids, light boxes, origami paper, papier-mache paste, rub-on graphics, stencils and templates, velcro, and so on. But the beginner needs no more than the simple, basic items mentioned above.

Source Materials: An Exhibit Bookshelf

Several how-to books offer more complete instruction on creating exciting exhibits. They provide examples of layout and design features, lists of supplies, sample projects, and other helpful information.

Mark Schaeffer's book, *Library Displays Handbook* is one of the most complete books on the subject that includes easy, step-by-step information on an array of design techniques. Full chapters are devoted to design lettering, illustration, construction signs, posters and wall displays, bulletin boards, and exhibits. In addition, Schaeffer provides excellent information about sources of material as well as extensive, up-to-date information on appropriate commercial software for various types of personal computers. Prices of software are included along with the addresses of suppliers. The suggested reading list has sections for calligraphy, computer graphics and desktop publishing, design, drawing, library displays, library public relations, and much more.

A complete exhibit reference bookshelf may also include other useful books:

Stephanie Borgwardt, *Library Display* (Johannesburg: Witwatersrand University Press, 1970).

Originally published in 1960, it remains modern in coverage of the theory and principles of library display; good analysis of what makes exhibits successful with lots of examples from the Library of Congress and elsewhere.

Linda Campbell Franklin, *Display and Publicity Ideas for Libraries* (Jefferson, NC: McFarland and Company, 1985).

Provides a list of display ideas and a month-by-month calendar of exhibit themes; includes how-to instructions for a wide range of sample exhibits.

Mona Garvey, *Library Displays: Their Purpose, Construction, and Use* (New York: The H.W. Wilson Company, 1969).

Includes a good section on how exhibits impact library use.

Alan Heath, *Off The Wall: The Art of Book Display* (Littleton, CO: Unlimited, 1987).

Provides information on design techniques; sample projects; resource lists.

Rita Kohn, *Experiencing Displays* (Metuchen, NJ: The Scarecrow Press, Inc. 1982).

Variety of projects presented; helpful glossary of design terminology.

Alan Swann, *How to Understand and Use Design and Layout* (Cincinnati: North Light Books, 1987).

Demonstrates how the function of design is to communicate; provides excellent instruction on how to use basic elements of design; good examples of professional design projects with production details.

REFERENCES

1. Mark Schaeffer, *Library Displays Handbook* (New York: H. W. Wilson, 1991), p.v.
2. Ibid., p. 18.
3. Ibid., p. 19.
4. Ibid., p. 11.

Index

Bridging funds, 69
Interviewing, 67-68
Job counseling, 69
Outreach techniques, 67
Position descriptions, 66
Recommendation/personnel
    review, 68
Selection criteria, 66-67
Training/intern programs, 69-70
Training support, 69
Travel to recruit, 70
*Reference Encyclopedia of the
    American Indian*, 198
Research support, 166-169
Retention, 70-74
    Barriers to success, 71-72
    Create supportive climate, 71-73
    Educate staff, 73
Roles/responsibility—Staff, 27-29
Roosevelt, Franklin D., 37-38

S

Schaeffer, Mark, 202
Schwartz, Diane, 178
*The Seven Habits of Highly Effective
    People*, xi
Smith, C. H. Erskine, 52
Society of Women Engineers,
    182
SRRT, 1
Staff development, 73-74
Steelworkers (USA) v Weber,
    433-US-193, 59
Stoffle, Carla, 27
Strategic planning, 24-27
Strategic vision, 24
Summer Bridge Program, 159
Supervision, 131-148
    Flexibility, 135
    Learning to change, 134-135
    Relinquishing authority, 135
    Workplace culture, 135-136
        Communication, 139-145
        Evaluating performance,
            143-144

Fostering staff relations,
    144-145
Orientation and training,
    136-139, 142
Problems, 145-148
Professionalism, 145
Realistic/clear expectations,
    143
Workplace environment,
    133-134
Cooperation, 134
Goals/expectations, 134
Open communication, 133
Self-actualization, 134
Shared decision-making,
    133-134
Trust, 133
Supervision problems
    Facing reality, 148
    Reducing the odds, 146
    Respect, 148
    Sound relations with personnel,
        146-147
    Understanding feelings of staff
        member, 147
Supervisor—characteristics, 132-133

T

*Teaching Strategies for Ethnic
    Studies*, 190
Total quality management, 32-34
Training/Intern Program, 73
Truman, Harry, 38

U

*Understanding Asian Americans: A
    Curriculum Resource Guide*,
    190
Unemployment Relief Act, 37
*Uniform Guidelines on Employment
    Selection Procedures*, 53
US Department of Labor, 40-41, 43
University of California at
    Berkeley, 5